Forew

I was delighted to be asked to write the foreword to this book. Maybe they told me to just write "four words" but in true Ken Dodd fashion, why use four words when four hundred will do?

This book is a great tribute, written with huge affection and rightly so, for a very special man. It's about chance meetings, stories from fans and from people who simply adored the man, just like I did. Ken strongly valued his privacy but he gave so much of himself to people. Doddy touched our hearts, our lives and especially our "chuckle muscles". People thought they "knew" Ken Dodd because he was so genuine, there was absolutely no side to him. But I was one of the privileged few who got to know the real Ken Dodd, the private Ken Dodd, the Ken Dodd who to me was an even better friend than he was an entertainer - and he was the greatest entertainer in the world!

I have always believed that there are two types of comedians. Those who say things funny and those who say funny things. It's only the slightest change in the order of the words but one which makes a world of difference in reality. Whatever Tommy Cooper said would seem funny, he could read a shopping list and you would think it was funny because he said things funny. The other side as an example would be the great Bob Monkhouse who would say the most exquisitely funny things but not always naturally funny in himself. Sir Ken Dodd was the only comedy performer I have ever seen with *both* attributes to perfection. He would say things funny and say funny things.

I knew Ken for most of my life. My dad George was a magician and ventriloquist in the Merseyside clubs and would

Cont.

often appear on the same shows as Doddy, even including a show that became quite famous when the Beatles and Ken Dodd performed on the same Liverpool variety show, with Ken topping the bill of course!

When I became a comedian in the early 1980's who better to learn from and get advice than the maestro himself? And learn I did. Every moment I spent in the company of Sir Ken Dodd was a masterclass in the art and craft of comedy. He devoted hour upon hour of his precious time analysing comedy, my act, offering me advice and teaching me the ropes. I once had the most incredible experience in my learning curve.

After one of the many shows we worked together, I gave him a lift home. We arrived at Knotty Ash around 3am and in typical Doddy fashion, despite my protestations, he insisted I came in for a cup of tea. Then, sitting in his kitchen, he spent the next hour or more giving me the most incredible one-to-one comedy masterclass, explaining the different types of comedy and telling me how he always believed there was *"is comedy"* and *"was comedy"* drawing out on paper the differences and how to approach each type.

Knowing I was also an aspiring joke writer, he explained how there always had to be the right amount of words in a joke to make it work, one word too many or one not enough would made the joke not right. He told me a joke was like a song, there had to be a beat and a rhythm to it. "Young man" he said "You don't tell a joke, you sing a joke!"

I felt so privileged to receive this advice but that was Doddy. He often put me in experiences where I felt privileged. He spoke about me on the famous Parkinson television chat show, he invited me to come and see his statue being unveiled at Liverpool's Lime Street Station and he even spent ages giving

Cont.

ABSENT FRIENDS

A Tribute to Sir Ken Dodd

by

Mike Bartram

Grosvenor House
Publishing Limited

This book is published by
Grosvenor House Publishing Ltd
Link House
140 The Broadway, Tolworth, Surrey, KT6 7HT.
www.grosvenorhousepublishing.co.uk

A CIP record for this book
is available from the British Library

ISBN 978-1-78623-323-3

Laughter is the greatest music in the World and audiences come to my shows to escape the cares and worries of everyday life. They don't want to be embarrassed or insulted. They want to laugh and so do I...which is probably why it works!

Sir Ken Dodd

Susan & Shelia Callaghan 1965

me a tour backstage of the London Palladium regaling me with stories of some of the stars that had appeared there

We would have late night chats on the phone, sometimes way after midnight. He asked me to come with him on his 80th birthday to unveil a plaque at Liverpool's Royal Court Theatre. Afterwards, Ken, his beloved partner Anne and myself stood in the middle of busy Williamson Square in the centre of Liverpool eating doughnuts. Here was a man who had smashed box office records at the London Palladium, who was revered the length and breadth of the country but he was just as happy to spend his special birthday eating doughnuts from a paper bag!

I also became one of his regular joke writers and though he was an exacting taskmaster, knowing exactly what he wanted and most importantly *when* he wanted it, the whole experience of writing jokes for Ken Dodd was an honour I can only compare to being asked to mix the paints for Van Gogh! It was that big for me and when I got it right and he gave me a look or a nod, then I felt 10 feet tall. I wrote for some of his major television and radio appearances. It was hard graft but he would encourage me non-stop. Occasionally, he wouldn't fancy a particular joke but I did, I thought the line had merit, and I would push and push for it. It was risky but if it worked, he would give me that wonderful nod of approval. I remember one show in Warrington and one particular joke we almost argued about back stage.

Ken was adamant it was not right but, in the end, I said "do it". Well, he did the gag and it got a big laugh and even a round of applause. I was watching from the wings and straight after the joke he actually stopped the show and told the whole packed theatre that it was my joke, what had happened earlier backstage and that I was watching from the wings. What an honour, I could almost cry with pride even now when I recall it. "Son" he would say to me "Most comics can't write jokes

Cont.

and most writers can't be comics...but you are different to them, you can do both!" My heart would beat out of my chest. I know that he often asked a mutual friend "How is the apprentice doing?" meaning me. Wonderful

Over the years from what I saw, Ken was the most generous person in the world with his time. Audiences still talk about the length of his stage shows but what not everyone knows, is that he would do another 2 hours in the dressing room afterwards, talking and joking with people. People always felt like they knew him as he was so friendly. He would stop and talk to everyone he met, would spend hours backstage or at the stage door with people and always carried a pile of photographs in his pocket so that anyone who wanted one would get a signed picture.

I remember he said to me not that long ago how he thought it was unusual that people had smartphones and didn't ask for autographs but instead wanted a photograph with him. But again, everyone who wanted one, he would readily oblige. He was such a people's person and would make no distinction from Prime Ministers down to the youngest trainee waiter or waitress. A wonderful example of a human being. He even came to my old school to present prizes to pupils just because I asked him to.

Ken was a real animal lover and especially dogs. He absolutely loved them. He always asked about mine. He was also so charming and polite to my wife whenever we all met up. For years, he only ever called my wife Lady Joanne even though she is a mere Joanne!

When he told me he was getting a Knighthood I asked him "What do I call you now? Is it Sir Ken all the time?" We both laughed and agreed that "Sir Doddy" might be appropriate.

This Knighthood, I know meant the world to him and it was just recognition for someone who was the best in their business.

Cont.

One of the nicest things I was able to do for him was when I arranged as a surprise to have the great Jimmy Tarbuck pay a visit to Ken's Good Turns Christmas lunch a couple of years ago. Ken and Jimmy had not been in touch for a long time and Jimmy, who I also wrote jokes for, always asked about him. In the end I said "Jimmy, come and see him" and he did. Ken was delighted and so was I. I managed to get what I think is my favourite photograph, one I only dreamt of ever getting, with Ken, Jimmy and myself

I was with Sir Ken for his 90th birthday celebrations. His beloved Good Turns Society, a charity he formed to help smaller charities, threw a terrific birthday party for him. He was in good health and I know he had a wonderful night. I was also privileged to work on his last major production, a BBC Radio 4 Extra about his life to celebrate his 90th birthday. I even got to ask him a couple of questions on the show.

A 90th birthday is such a big milestone and I struggled to know what you would get someone like him as a present. I had collected 1600 joke books since I was a kid, we were downsizing our house and the timing was perfect. I went over in a friend's van to Knotty Ash and his face just lit up when he saw all these joke books. He adored comedy books anyway and I absolutely scored a bull's eye with these. Poor Lady Anne didn't know what to say or where they would go, but he was absolutely in his element, like a kid on Christmas morning. Fantastic.

In the December I visited him in his home and it was clear he wasn't well. But we had a lovely long chat, with him reminiscing and I made him laugh with a few stories of where I had been recently and the shows I had performed on. Sadly, this was the last time I was to see him. He was admitted to hospital only two weeks later

Not long before he was discharged from hospital we had a long chat on the 'phone, he was in his hospital bed. He told

Cont.

me how he was struggling with his walking, and we spent a long time talking about how we might restructure his act, using an armchair with him regaling the audience with stories. I am sure he believed it wholeheartedly and he would have been sensational at it, with audiences queuing round the block. "Doddy sitting down" I told him "Just imagine how long the shows could go on for then!" and he had a good old chuckle at that one.

Merseyside loved him, showbusiness loved him and I loved him. He was a very special, loyal and trusted friend to me for more than 35 years. On 28th March 2018 I had the sad but proud honour of being one of the pallbearers at Ken's funeral. Tears were streaming down my face but it was a role I was privileged to do for him

I genuinely believe that Sir Ken Dodd was the greatest theatre comedian the world has ever seen. I feel very proud that he was my friend.

Ken, thank you for being such a big part of my life and of course, such a big part of the lives of the fans, some of whom have shared their stories and memories of the great man in this lovely book.

John Martin

Liverpool

www.johnmartincomedy.com

Introduction

I remember seeing Ken Dodd as a child, I would have been about 10 years old, he was performing at Hindley Monaco and my Grandparents took me along. I remember how excited I was at being allowed to stay out past midnight! Never imagining that 28 years later I would have the privilege of sharing some special, dear moments in the company of the great man himself and would still be out past midnight!

Famous for his late finishes, he was the worst nightmare of some house managers. Before I first worked with Ken I was at a House Manager's Forum and the subject came up, how do you get him off stage? One House Manager told me that she brought the house tabs in on him but he just stepped in front of them and carried on! Another told me that he threw the keys at Ken and said, "if you're thinking of staying on till 1am, you can lock up yourself" whether these anecdotes are true or not I don't know but I knew that I couldn't do this to Ken.

On his first performance with me as House Manager he came along and shook my hand, "Ah you're the new broom" he exclaimed, "don't worry, I'll be out early" I watched the show from the wing, taking me back to my ten-year-old self, but this time he was only feet away, I was witnessing the mechanics of the show from a privileged angle. The show finished at around ten past midnight, Ken came off stage and went off to the dressing room, about an hour later I could hear him coming down the stairs. Concerned that he sounded like he was struggling, I went and found him fighting with a dirty great suitcase, "what on earth are you doing?" I quizzed, "we have to be out quick, don't we?" he asked. "Listen Ken, I'll be here for all your shows and I'll look after you, you take as long as

Cont.

you need" he smiled, gave me the suitcase and returned to his dressing room, our relationship had been cemented and he did take his time!

Over the years we became friends, chatting after his shows about the business, his thoughts on variety and he always wanted to know what I'd been up to in the year since we'd last seen each other. Ken would sit in dressing room number 1, his dressing room at the Grand (and always will be) I'd offer him a drink from the bar, he always refused, preferring instead to drink his can of lager from a plastic beaker.

Last year I told him that my Grandfather had been unwell and that he needed an operation on his heart, the following week Ken called me up to his dressing room and gave me a get well soon card, "To the Great Frank, wishing you health and happiness, Ken Dodd" and the Dicky Mint drawing, I was blown away and so was the Great Frank!

There'd always be a queue of people outside stage door with things they'd like to get signed and we would take them up to Kens room where he'd sit and sign it all, often during our chats, then myself or Lady Anne would take them back for the waiting fans, some would leave happy that they'd got their memorabilia signed, others would wait determined that no matter how late it was they were going to speak with Ken and he would never disappoint. Normally around 3am Ken would come down, we'd chat a little just inside stage door, he would enquire what we had on that week, often having to sign a few extra bits as we spoke, then he'd go out to speak to his public.

Some nights I'd see Ken, "pressing the flesh" for a solid hour, having pictures taken with people, signing bits and pieces and he wouldn't get into the car until he'd spoken to every one of them. One night, I recall a young lad waiting outside to meet his hero, he was about 18 and wanted to be a stand-up comedian,

Cont.

Ken spent 30 minutes offering him advice, told him to send his material to him, he would give him some pointers

The last time he performed at the Grand, he was out there for a good forty minutes, on a cold November night, it was easy to forget that Ken was 90 and had just done a marathon show.

On the last show of every run, I would present Ken with a little something as a thank you, always four cans of his favourite lager and a box of chocolates for Lady Anne. The last time I saw him, we did the usual exchange of gifts and Ken proudly presented me with a bottle of malt whiskey, he shook my hand and thanked me for my friendship.

I have been lucky enough to have spent time in the presence of this Great man. A wonderful, caring man, who always seemed genuinely interested in what anybody had to say, who cared, who listened and who understood. I shall miss those magical, special moments that we shared each October and I shall cherish the memories forever.

Shaun Gorringe
House Manager. The Grand Blackpool

We first met Ken in 1965 at the age of 6. Our mother took us to Beatties store in Birkenhead where Ken was officially opening their new record department. Our mother told us we queued for an hour or more and when he arrived he spotted us in the crowd and he asked my Mum if he could have his picture taken with us for the Liverpool Echo.

Of course Mum said yes and from that moment on my twin and I (christened by Ken as The Diddy Twins) and our little sister Karen became lifelong fans. Our Mum would take us to see his shows and pantomimes in Liverpool and Blackpool and each time he would allow us backstage for a photo and a giggle. When our Mum passed away from breast cancer when we were 13yrs old and our little sister Karen just 10, he wrote the loveliest letter to us which we have never forgotten. As we all grew up we kept going to see Ken's shows. It may sound a little strange but every time we went we felt closer to our Mum.

Each time we would go to see his show we were allowed back stage to see him. (Anne you were always so lovely to us too). Ken would always make time to have a laugh with us and although it was very late he would chat away to us like he had all the time in the world. Genuinely interested in our lives and how we were getting on.

Our last meeting was at a charity event last year at the Hilton in Liverpool for Herbert of Liverpool (a dear friend of ours). Ken was presented with a cake for his 90th birthday and he offered it for auction to raise money for Marie Curie Cancer Care. We bought the cake and it's still looking pretty fabulous on display at my friend's shop in Parkgate Wirral.

Cont.

There will never be another like him and we feel so lucky and grateful to have had a little piece of him in our lives. We'll treasure our photographs of our first meeting when we were 6yrs old – the original photos we gave to Ken a few years ago.

Once again, our hearts go out to Lady Anne and all the family.

R.I.P. Sir Kenneth Arthur Dodd. Squire of Knotty Ash and a REAL Gentleman. We will never forget you xxx

Susan Callaghan

This is of the time when the national anthem was played at the end of every theatre performance or cinema programme. Some people used to try to duck out before it started, especially if they were trying to catch a late bus, for once it started you had to stand where you were.

Its summer 1968 and Ken is at the Opera House for the season. It's the second half of the show and Ken's onstage, singing. Time's getting on a bit. End of the song, Ken looks at his watch, straightens up and buttons his jacket and stands to attention at the mike. The house lights come on and the stewards open the exits. The audience are taken aback by the sudden end of the show and are quickly gathering children, jackets etc. More than a few are already through the exits. There's a drum roll and the 'national anthem' starts.... Happiness, happiness and the exits are slammed shut. For about a second there's silence then the loudest roar of laughter I've ever heard in a theatre. The place is a shambles but the show continues for another 10-15 minutes, and those who left don't get back in!

Years later I thanked Ken for giving me the best laugh I'd ever had in a theatre. He asked what that was and when I told him he laughed at the memory and said "You should have seen it from the stage, 3 floors of chaos!" The great thing was, each audience was asked not to give the game away and nobody did in our hotel anyway.

Sandra Wallace

Ken was so full of love.

Love for his craft, for the business, for comedy, for his family, his home, Liverpool, his dogs, his fans but, above all, for Anne. His true Lady.

We hope all our love we had back for him is truly felt by his family, close friends and Anne.

We are truly blessed to have had such a star shine on earth. Now he shines forever above us all.

Rachel Lewin, Biggleswade xxx

Took my Mum to see Ken at Nottingham last year. Unfortunately we had to leave half way through as my Mum was unwell. We wrote to Ken as we felt sad we had to leave such a fantastic show. We were so happy to receive a lovely letter from him and a personalised photograph of himself to each of us which we treasure. This reflects what a lovely man he was - finding the time to write to us. We love him immensely and he will be greatly missed. Each time we look at his photograph it brings HAPPINESS to us all.

Denise, Beryl (Mum) and Kate

To Lady Anne and Sir Ken's Family and all the Diddy Men from Knotty Ash.

Doddy, thank you for the laughter, smiles and tickling sticks you have given for many, many years. Heaven is now blessed with you, here in our city of Liverpool and the University of

Cont.

Knotty Ash you will always be in the hearts of the people who loved your sense of humour there will never be another Doddy like Sir Kenneth Arthur Dodd OBE.

Ally Woods

I had the pleasure of meeting and spending time with Sir Ken. He was the greatest comedian / entertainer of all time. He brought happiness to everyone he met both young and old. I remember us walking from the theatre to McDonald's it was hilarious as everyone shouted there greetings to him. He has now gone to his greatest audience in heaven to entertain. Condolences to Anne.

David G Smith

I had the honour and privilege to see Ken perform on a number of occasions over the years, most memorably at the reopening of the Leeds City Varieties.

He was simply the greatest there has ever been and a true gentleman.

Sincere condolences to his wife, family circle and the people of Liverpool.

Mark D Lawlor (Dundonald, N Ireland)

I so miss my wonderful dear friend who for 47 years was my friend till the 11th March. I was sat 4 chairs behind Roy at the funeral in the cathedral. I hope you're finding all your friends and family up in Heaven.

Vera Yorke

For a birthday treat for my late sister-in-law whose birthday fell on the 28th of December we surprised her with tickets for my wife and myself and her (Margaret) to see Sir Ken's annual Christmas show at the Philharmonic Hall, Hope Street, Liverpool. We arrived early to take our seats and I secretly passed a note via the stage door for a request for a birthday mention.

In the interval Sir Ken kindly obliged looking at the scrap of paper he announced "We have a birthday to announce this evening, where are you Margaret Carlyle?" Margaret up in the circle far too shy to answer, fell silent, so I bellowed "Up here!!" And faster than the speed of light Sir Ken retorted "Dear dear Margaret do you have a sore throat, have you been ill??" A cherished memory

John Grant

When I saw him at Xmas at the end of the show Ken just sat on his chair and was talking to the audience as if we were just having a cup of tea, that was the real Ken in my eyes and his parting words were 'people ask me why I carry on and I tell them I carry on for all of you'.

Tina Molloy

Cont.

The last of the TRUE comedy legends in my opinion, first saw Doddy in 66? I think the year's right at the Stockport Gaiety Club, last saw him in Southport 2006 absolute genius God bless and thank you x

Mark Sheenan

A few years ago when I saw Doddy in Knotty Ash Sainsbury's I would introduce him to my young daughters, Ken always greeted them with a warm, friendly 'Hello' I would tell my girls they had just met the greatest Liverpudlian ever and the funniest!! They were too young to understand at the time!

2 years ago, my daughter was working in a Restaurant in Childwall. Doddy was a regular there, polite and charming as usual to everyone.

One night he said to my daughter 'By Jove you're pretty, if we were in Egypt now I could trade you for 3 camels' in a quick one liner he made people laugh and my daughter feel special in an instant, isn't that our hero all over?

When my daughter told me about this encounter in the Restaurant, I said to her 'what did I tell you all those years ago'?

Mike Bartram

The King of Laughter and Song

For decades and decades Doddy entertained us

No one cared if they missed the last bus.

Lots of laughs and some great songs too

He made us happy like no other comedian could do.

The Diddymen were such good fun

And laughed along to every Doddy pun.

No one could tell jokes like our beloved Ken

So much laughter came from his pen.

Now he's gone up to the sky

We still wonder 'why oh why'

But over the years he was the best

How he deserves his eternal rest.

His jokes will live forever more

The number one star eternally on his door.

Stephen Ashfield

'What a Beautiful Day!'

What a beautiful day for Heaven to go.
And perform a special one man show.
All my absent friends I have got to see.
They were there to hug and greet me.

What a beautiful day for Heaven to go.
My journeys end down on Earth below.
But by Jove what a journey I can boast!
I even married the one who I loved most.

What a beautiful day for Heaven to go.
Happiness galore, no gales to blow.
Just Angels, sunshine under skies of blue.
My faith rewarded, my dream come true.

Mike Bartram

So sorry to read of Ken's passing. I literally grew up knowing Ken Dodd because my grandfather David Forester was his agent for many years. Whenever my sister and I visited our grandparents, Grandpa would often be on the phone to Ken, listening, counselling and negotiating. We also had the pleasure of being taken to the shows.

To this day even with all the great stand-ups we have, no comedian has been able to deliver the intensity of that mass visceral laughter that was Ken's hallmark - it was almost physically painful to experience. It wasn't just the jokes but his clownish presence and the riveting rapport as he looked around the auditorium, winding his hair up into a sticky steeple declaring "How tickled I am," and enquiring "Are you tickled Mrs?"

The variety theatre was his natural playground, one that he graced with extraordinary talent. To claim there will never be his like again might sound like a cliché but one that is uniquely applicable to Ken Dodd.

With condolences to Anne.

Greg Spiro

Cont.

To Lady Anne

I was sorry to learn that Sir Ken had passed away. I offer my sympathy and prayers for you at this sad time. I remember meeting Sir Ken at the St John's Knotty Ash Garden Fete, which he opened, and how Sir Ken took the time to speak to the people who were enjoying the event. I shall remember you in my prayers. Knotty Ash will never be the same without Sir Ken., who made people happy and had a great sense of humour and a great singing voice.

Yours **Barry Souster**

We won't forget you ken you made us laugh and now you made us cry for the loss of you!! Never forgotten you will live in our hearts forever. Thanks for making us howl with laughter R.I.P

Corinne and Stewart

Tatty Bye Squire!!

It's not a day for the Diddy Men to weep.

Doddy's only in heaven having a sleep.

The squire's having a rest by Gods side.

Making the angels laugh until they cried.

But something *does* feel missing from L14

A light gone out, a blank stage and screen.

Now the Liverpool streets, thousands line.

As the 2 horses trot slowly in perfect time.

The early rain and the hail it couldn't deter.

The people of Knotty Ash standing there.

The gift of laughter Doddy has left behind

We'll laugh forever as he was one of a kind.

So today all you Diddy men, no need to cry.

Just think 'HAPPINESS' and smile tatty bye!

Mike Bartram

No More Doddy

Goodbye Doddy, we all miss you so.
You made me laugh, when feeling low.
Had me laughing since I was small.
Could make anyone feel 10 feet tall.

'Never meet your heroes' they say.
But I met Doddy one summer day.
Humble and funny, the perfect gent.
I felt so honoured, when away I went!

Now I pass your home as I often do.
I look at the many tributes left for you.
Flowers and cards drenched in rain.
No more Doddy at the window pane.

Every fan has a similar story to share.
How Ken never lacked respect and care.
Off stage too the greatest until the end.
Now left with our very own 'absent friend'.

Mike Bartram

I remember attending one of Ken's shows in Southport, on the way out, I walked behind a family, two parents and a teenage girl, and I heard the girl say. 'Mum I'm so glad you dragged me here to listen to Ken I haven't had as much fun in ages, when are we coming again' I thought that was fantastic, Ken gaining young fans all the time!

Irene Walsh

He was a wonderful down to earth man, no airs and graces, full of life and love for all who crossed his path. Miss you darling Doddy xxx

Enid Marl

I would like to share my memories of Ken Dodd. My husband and I went to see him every year and laughed and laughed. He certainly was a tonic for us. We met him on 2 occasions and he was a lovely man, despite asking my husband at the time we met him at the Royal Court theatre 'are you on the run from weightwatchers?' Haha We were devastated at his death and left a book and poem outside his house as a personal memento. His funeral was fitting for a king of comedy.

RIP Sir Ken remembered always.

Christine and Gerry Barnes

Sir Ken was a wonderful man and always had time for the fans. Met him a few times over the years but we will never forget him.

Val, Alan & Mike.xxx Valerie Watkins

Cont.

Ken used to play certain venues at the same time each year and once fans saw the date they would book up. Ken did a lot of the same material and would make a joke about it, as Ricky Tomlinson said in a programme about Doddy last year. Where some comedians would do a new show each tour, Ken just added to his material so the shows got longer and longer.

Mark Wakeman

Today as I was out walking with my Mum we started talking about Ken. Within seconds a double rainbow appeared...I guess he is watching over us all. Miss him so much.

Linda Patricia Thomas

I must say there is no other comic that I would travel from Caterham to Worthing for to see in concert. But I was happy to so for our Doddy! He was, and is a one of a kind.

Mr Alan Penfold

My story and memory of Ken is...

As a child at home in the 50's, Ken Dodd was a regular on the television. We used to see him on the variety shows and also on Sunday night at the London Palladium. In the early 60's, Ken's records were often being played on our radiogram. I didn't really take much interest at that time where music was concerned. But, as a teenager, especially in 1964 I followed most of the groups and bought their records.

In 1965 Ken Dodd hit the charts in the UK with "Tears" and remained at the top of the charts at number one for five weeks. I can remember being told that in a few years' time most of these singers of today wouldn't last, but Ken Dodd will still be performing all around the Country for his audiences. And he certainly was. How true those words were.

It was quite a few years later when I started to go and see Ken Dodd at the theatres around the UK. It was a treat to see him and enjoy his long shows that he was famous for. I saw him in York, Buxton and Torquay a few times. Then I noticed my local theatre, The Garrick in Lichfield Staffordshire had got advertised tickets for Ken Dodd's Happiness show which was coming on sale for the following season. I bought tickets and got front row seats right in the middle. I was delighted! It seemed a long few months away, but then the time had come and I sat eagerly waiting in my seat for Doddy to come onto the stage. He came on to the tune of "Happiness" followed by a huge applause from the audience.

The show continued with Ken telling his jokes, singing in between, and then he came over to the edge of the stage and

Cont.

asked me what my name was! I told him it was Sandra, he then asked me if I was the romantic type, if I liked being wined and dined, did I like to receive flowers. I could see that there was a reason for all of this, and he knew I was willing to participate with him during his performance on stage. I was then mentioned a few times during some of the jokes he was telling. At some point he asked if I could swim because there would be no danger of me drowning! It was all good clean fun.

In the interval I had a few people come up to me and say how brave I was to sit there and go along with it all. It was all very funny and I was glad to have been chosen to take part. The second half continued and Ken brought me into his jokes during the 5 hours he was on stage. I was more than happy to have Doddy chat with me while on stage in front of a packed audience. This is something I would normally shy away from. But this was Doddy!

At the end of the show, Doddy came to the edge of the stage once again, but this time bent forward and handed me his Tickling Sticks and said "These are for you and thank you for being so kind".

The last time I saw Ken Dodd was at The Opera House in Buxton Derbyshire 2016, he was brilliant as always. I still have his Tickling Sticks he gave me when he was at The Garrick theatre in Lichfield. I will never part with them. I, like so many others will miss Sir Ken Dodd. Thanks Doddy you are a real National Treasure. You will always be remembered. Bless you Ken. Tatty bye Tatty bye.

Sandra Borgazzi

Doddy Poem

Thanks for all the happiness that you brought all your life.

I'm pleased that you finally made your partner Anne your wife!

So after all the years of laughter that you brought us all.

Now it's time for reflection and wasn't it a ball!!

A special man in every way who came from Knotty Ash.

And like all the Diddy men he always had a bash.

His shows went on for hours with the humour he'd create.

And everybody knew that they would arrive home very late!!

Always in a taxi cos the last bus went hours ago.

Everybody knew the script when you went to Ken's Happiness show.

So when he banged upon the Knotty Ash Drum your attention he did grab.

But every show was magical and in the swinging 60's he was Fab!!

He was filled with plumshusness and discomknockerated too.

A master of his craft to bring his Happiness to You.

So as the final curtain falls on the Legend Sir Kenneth Arthur Dodd.

Cont.

Heaven TV will have the show "Sir Ken Dodd's audience with God!" !!

By jove Doddy we will all miss you and your infectious humour. R.I.P Tatty Bye Sir Ken

Fan's Tribute

I have lovely memories of Sir Ken going back to 1976 when I was about 10 years of age and bumping into him at a local butcher in Stoneycroft with my Mum, this memory always stirs up the first joke I ever heard ... Ken asking for scraps for his dog and his Diddymen shouting with glee "ooh goody we're getting a dog!!"

I had the privilege of bumping into him or passing him by in and who'd have thought that both of my sons would end up being one of his paper boys... one job I won't forget as occasionally my husband and I would take pity on the boys and DO their round for them (more so when the weather was bad) and boy did we know when we had Sir Ken's papers, he always asked for them to be placed in a bag hanging on the inside of his open porch ... hardly surprising really as it had THREE of the largest papers i.e. The Guardian, Observer and Times along with all their Magazine supplements ... who would want that lot thumping through their letterbox at 8.30 on a Sunday Morning!

My proudest moment was when my eldest got to meet Sir Ken personally, it was one Christmas Day after the Eucharist Service, my Son was a Chorister with the Anglican Cathedral and was over the moon to have his photo taken and after watching some of Sir Ken's shows he has become a firm fan proving that Sir Ken's humour has no age limit and will continue down the years for eternity.

Whilst I was chatting to my husband about Ken's tribute book he pass remarked how he loved chatting to Sir Ken on Christmas Days in the Anglican Cathedral and on one occasion after introducing Sir Ken to our Son Thomas in his Choir

Cont.

Robes, Sir Ken said that he loved coming to Cathedral and he was very proud of the Choir if not a little envious as he himself had been knocked back to join being advised he wasn't good enough .He did also add that he was in good company as Sir Paul McCartney also got knocked back from joining the Cathedral Choir too!

Just goes to show eh, even talented singers like Sir Ken and Sir Paul don't necessarily get all the breaks!

Debbie Fisher xx

The world is a poorer place with the death of Doddy on March 11th. What an amazing man, generous to a fault and extremely talented. My husband and I saw him a few years back in Liverpool. We have never laughed so much and for so long! I watched him on TV when growing up in Liverpool over many years. Will really miss him as will all Liverpool people in particular. He was truly unique. Condolences to his wonderful wife.
Love you Doddy

Sue Lowe. QLD Australia

We older ones were privileged to live the entirety of Our Ken's era, now at an end. R.I.P. Ken; be seeing you soon enough! Warmest regards

John Kelly, in Caracas

Sir Ken, it was a pleasure to know you, you were a comic genius so clever and true. You sang like a lark and had much success. You were a gentleman in every sense of the word. You will be sorely missed by all. May you rest in peace. Deepest condolences to Lady Anne.

**Jill McIntosh and Lynn James
Helpers at Chord Theatrical Agency**

You will be greatly missed by the press photographers of Merseyside.

David Kendall

Cont.

Sir Ken you will be sadly missed by the whole of Liverpool, you were a legend, a gentleman, and one of the nicest people I have ever met, you always had time for all, your shows you gave extra time, my father in-law Ken was a true fan, he's in heaven to, hope you meet up, all the angels are your audience now, good night and God bless we will miss you.

Mr and Mrs Cook

Ken Dodd Poem

When I heard Sir Ken had died
I just sat down and cried and cried.
Then I thought of Lady Anne
Who had just married this great man.

What a loss it must have been
He was her King and she was his Queen.
Her life with Ken was happy and fun
And he was loved by everyone.

But she was the one who captured his heart
For 40 years till death they did part.
By his side every day
Whether it was for work or play.

Sir Ken was a man so gentle and kind
With a lovely smile and a brilliant mind.
I loved him myself I must confess
He brought me such joy and happiness.

I am so happy that before he died
He asked Anne to be his bride.
Forever now he'll be in her heart
And they will never be apart.

Rest in Peace Sir Ken Dodd. You were a wonderful human
being and an example to us all
Thanks for the memories

Jan Rawlings

Dicky Mint

Your little friend Dicky Mint
Makes everybody smile.
You hold him close, bring him to life
Just for a little while.

The power of speech is yours to give
And this you do with love.
It's obvious to all who watch
He was given from above.

He means so very much to you
He brings you so much joy.
You share him happily with us
This cheeky little boy.

To you he is not made of wood
He is very real indeed.
If you could give him breath you would
He fills in you a need.

He helps to fill a space
Deep inside your heart.
He keeps a smile upon your face
We know you'll never part.

So from all of us that love you
To both of you we say.
Happiness and laughter
for ever and a day.

By Rosemarie Jones (2006)

Best ever comedian in my mind.

Year after year he left all behind!

Jovial, cheerful, born with a smile.

One off comic, unique in style.

Vivacious, so amazing for his age.

Ever the thinker, ever the sage.

Made Knotty Ash a famous place.

Incredible delivery, lightening pace!

Stayed loyal to his roots and home.

Surpassed by nobody, out on his own.

Ultimate professional year after year.

Spread eternal happiness and cheer!

Mike Bartram

Dear Anne and family

After shedding so many tears of happiness at watching Ken's shows, we now find ourselves shedding tears of sadness at his passing.

We saw him at the City Varieties in Leeds a few years ago and were literally on the edge of our seats with laughter. When I wrote a note, to tell him that Stephanie, my partner and ardent Ken Dodd fan, was ill and couldn't go to one of his shows, he sent her a tickling stick and a signed autograph.

Ken was a phenomenon, a one off, a ventriloquist, singer with an operatic voice and master of the one liner. He bottled happiness and gave it to everyone he met and his laughter will echo long after his passing.

God is now the benefactor of his one line humour, and Heaven will not rest in peace if Ken has anything to do with it.

God bless you Ken.

From Paul and Stephanie (Leeds, Yorkshire)

Xxx

We were so very sad to hear of the death of Sir Ken Dodd ("Doddy") on Sunday. Ken was a legend - the last of the great stand-up music hall entertainers. We started going to his "Happiness Shows" more than 30 years ago and have followed him all over the country - sometimes seeing four or five shows in a single year. He always noticed us if we were sitting in the front row, and addressed several jokes in our direction.

Cont.

We met him on a number of occasions and he was such a lovely man. Our thoughts go out to his wife, Lady Anne Dodd, at this difficult time. Doddy will be sadly missed, and there is no-one, but no-one, who can ever replace him. The world is a sadder place now that he is gone. Our sincere condolences.

Terry and Dorit. Moody Great Bookham

I met Doddy at Liverpool Cathedral carol concert four years ago.

He signed my programme to Ted and Jean asking who was Jean, I said that's my missus.

Ken immediately replied "Wives are wonderful - where would we be without them- I quite fancy the Bahamas!"

What a star, we loved him and always will. There'll be plumshusness by the bucket load in Heaven.

Take a well-earned rest Sir Ken, the greatest comedian of our time.

Your super fans Ted and Jean Towndrow

Hand in Hand

Irrelevant or insignificant the old days classed.

Dismissed far too often does become our past.

Buildings, places, stars of music, screen or stage.

You see them sadly resigned to a forgotten page.

It happens more and more, much to my dismay.

The past ignored, a distant memory, hazy or grey.

But our Doddy will never become a victim of this.

As such a legend would be impossible to dismiss.

Fashions, with time I've seen them come and go.

Trends, appear and vanish just like melting snow.

But the test of time our Doddy's legacy will stand.

As the future and Ken Dodd will go hand in hand.

Mike Bartram

The King of Entertainment

Played with Doddy to many a theatre packed.

One half of the funniest ever ventriloquist act.

But tonight Dicky Mint don't you feel too sad.

Think of the fantastic times that you both had!

Here's a thought, go out on the Town tonight!

Dazzle Liverpool dressed in your colours bright!

Raise a glass or two to Doddy while at the bar.

He was the King of Entertainment, a lasting star.

And you have your memories, we have ours too.

Doddy made me laugh, like only Doddy could do!

So tonight Dicky, toast Doddy with a rousing cheer.

And not with a shandy, have *that* 'bottle of beer'!

Mike Bartram

I had 2 of the original tickling sticks given to me by Ken when he appeared at our Hospital social club. He got me on the stage doing daft things, it was great. They disappeared when my girls were teenagers in 1980. I still have a later one which I treasure.

Phyllis Edwards

I was in a plaster cast from my thighs to my neck people used to stare...Ken looked into my eyes to speak to me he saw the person not the plaster cast. Oh he did sign it though when I asked politely only then did he ask what was wrong...

Linda Patricia Thomas

On the other side of the coin. I suffer from Eye Dystonia, most of the time my eyes are closed. At one show in Blackpool, I was sat in about the fourth row from the front, I was listening intently to Ken's every word, and then I heard him say 'I will keep you awake!' I opened my eyes to see him pointing to me.

Irene Walsh

I have two of the sheepskin type which have a plastic cover with the words Knotty Ash Tickling Stick printed on them. Also another which Ken signed the wooden handle. I will never part with any of them.

Stephen Windle

Cont.

Did you know Ken's parents had a holiday cottage in Penmachno North Wales Ken loved going there as a boy with his brother and sister they would go cycling, my late mother remembers them as she lived in Penmachno when she was young.

Ron Cross

I never got to see him live unfortunately, since his passing there has been an outpouring of love for him. I just hope he had a little inkling of how much he was loved and so respected.

Sheila Drew

Well, it's just over a year since I spent a happy half an hour with Ken Dodd backstage in Frome on 16th April 2017 (in fact 17th at 1am!). He offered me a beer - can of Carling. I said I'd drink from the can. He said "We're not hippies here, y'know!" and washed out a coffee cup for me in the sink!

We talked about comedy, cats (he had previously replied to be after I posted him my cat books A CAT CALLED DOG 1 and 2 by Jem Vanston), also Dennis Spicer, his ventriloquist friend who died in a head-on crash with my cousin in 1964. He looked very well and had done over 4 hours on stage! But I think one never knows when fate will strike for the very elderly - my mum also died recently, last December, but she was much frailer than Ken. We also chatted about the NHS of which my mum had both excellent and awful experiences.

Ken and Anne had a black poodle type dog with them - the latest of that breed they had owned - but they had once adopted a stray cat too. Ken had written to me previously after I posted him my A CAT CALLED DOG book in 2014 - he told me all about a stray cat they adopted (or who adopted the Dodds!) called Nellie. It was only after going to the vets that they found it was in fact NOT a female cat but a neutered tom! So Nellie became Herbert-Nellie - which could well make Ken a pioneer for transgender pets!

It's a shame he never got to record the song I wrote for him, but I shall treasure the memory of that night for the rest of my life - and follow his advice re comedy, showbiz, the BBC, Americans etc!

P.j. Vanston

I'd like to extend my sincere condolences to Lady Anne and all Sir Ken's family, close friends and many fans, in Liverpool and around the world, at this sad time.

I was born in 1965 at the peak of Ken's career and, it's fair to say, he was a constant throughout my life.

As a youngster I was regaled with tales of the Diddymen by my uncles, teenagers in the 60s who'd watched Ken's many TV shows and appearances and listened avidly to his radio shows encouraged by my grandparents, themselves fans.

As a teenager I was able to enjoy Ken's appearances first hand, whether tuning in to see him captivate the audience on Seaside Special or deliver his masterclass on the Good Old Days.

Like millions of us I was enthralled by his 'An Audience With...' a show I've wept with laughter watching all over again this evening.

As Ken slipped off the small screen, I resolved to see him at one of his many Happiness Show appearances up and down the country. It's to my eternal regret that, sadly, I left this too late. 'Life', I'm afraid, got in the way and by the time I made the booking (Gawsworth Hall later this year), well, the rest we know.

I've pondered this a great deal since we heard the sad news. For a short time I should confess that I let my frustration get the better of me; how could I have been so disorganised and why hadn't I just got my act together far enough in advance of the show selling out as they always did?

I've realised that these feelings were, to my shame, self-indulgent. The only sincere response at this time, along with

Cont.

the profound sadness which I know we all share, is to rejoice in the sheer joy which Ken exuded and to be grateful to have had the privilege to see him at all.

Like many others I marvelled at Ken's comic genius; there's no question that he was a master of his craft, one-of-a-kind who observed keenly and studied extensively, understanding more about human psychology than many eminent academics in the field.

What I'll remember Ken for though is his sheer humanity, his sincerity and the empathy he felt for all he came into contact with.

In footage this week I've heard Ken say many times that he was lucky; lucky not on account of his obvious success nor for enjoying the respect of his peers - which he undoubtedly did - but lucky simply to spend his time surrounded by happy people. It's a mark of the man that I believe he fervently believed this. I don't doubt that this is true but may I say that it is us, those who were privileged to witness this remarkable man, who are really the lucky ones.

May he rest in peace.

God bless.

Phil Burrow

Haslemere Surrey

The Milk Float Home

By the roadside holding out my thumb.
I heard the engine of a milk float hum.
'Any chance of a lift home please mate'
'I've been to a Doddy gig, no bus so late'!

And as the sun rose from the morning sky.
'Yes...jump on board' came the kind reply.
'Many thanks' I said,' I've not too far to go'
'It's always the same after a Doddy show'!

'I get home for breakfast, same for years'
'With the sound of laughter still in my ears'
In Knotty Ash, Doddys' home we passed.
So I jumped off nearby, I was home at last!

Mike Bartram

MEMORIES

Memories, we have them every day.

Everlasting, they can be here to stay.

Memories of Doddy, spring to mind.

Only happy memories most will find.

Reasons why he was the very best.

In entertainment, so ahead of the rest.

Enjoy your Doddy memories, as I do.

Save them in your heart, old and new.

Mike Bartram

KEN DODDY

Keep your absent friends laughing up above.

Every saddened fan, sends you hugs and love.

Nobody can replace our Doddy, it's an era end.

Diddymen left with Diddy hearts to mend.

Our hero is Doddy, in every sense of the word.

Doddy loved his fans, always showed he cared.

Down in my Knotty Ash, his legend will grow.

Young and old fans alike, love and miss you so.

Mike Bartram

As a Son of Liverpool and, in fact, Knotty Ash where I was born and lived until the age of 11/12 and attended Knotty Ash County Primary school, I recall often seeing Sir Ken around when he always had time for a friendly chat and would sometimes pop into my Dad's DIY shop for the odd item including paraffin.

In 1999 I became President of the Rotary Club of Heswall and chose Prostate Cancer Research Trust as my charity having lost my Dad to the condition a few years earlier. Sir Ken was at the charity launch at King's Dock when I approached him to ask if I could book him for a charity show. He agreed without hesitation offering his services free providing I found a venue and organised promotion and ticket sales.

I contacted the Gladstone Theatre, Port Sunlight, where Sir Ken had not previously performed, and offered a few dates to Lady Anne for Sir Ken to consider. Lady Anne was very cooperative and easy to deal with and confirmed a date very quickly for March 2000. Tickets sold out in no time and the show was terrific, finishing very late in true "Doddy" style! Sir Ken also brought several up and coming supporting entertainers into the show - yet another measure of his selflessness and the night made over £9,000 for Prostate Cancer Research Trust.

As a mark of appreciation in the show, when Lady Anne gave the go ahead after Sir Ken's routine, I presented him with a commemorative plaque from the Rotary Club and he was visibly quite touched. I shall be eternally grateful to Sir Ken giving his valuable time to a very worthy cause.

Cont.

Sir Ken Dodd was a true variety legend bringing happiness to so many people for so long.

Laughter is the best medicine and he created an abundance of it.

God bless him.

Derek Herbert

Fan's Tribute

October 1983 Ken came up to Fife to do a week at the Adam Smith Centre in Kirkcaldy. He asked to meet all the staff. Everybody. He gave each of them a tiny Diddyman's hat with an elastic chinstrap and asked them if they'd be his Diddymen for the week (no singing or dancing involved!) In return he gleaned the local info - where's the posh area, where's the best chip shop etc.

They thought he was priceless. Nice start, then Ken discovered he'd forgotten to bring shaving foam. Panic. It was 5.15 - where could he go? He ran down the path to the High Street and Woolworth's was nearest. 5 minutes to closing, he dodged the sentry at the door and got his shaving foam. Went to pay and didn't have change, only a £5 note. This news was not well received by the nippy assistant who had already cashed up and was having to get all her wee bags of coins out again to give Ken his change. She was extremely rude to him, involving a colleague in a shouted conversation across the shop.

She didn't know that the quiet man she was haranguing was taking it all in. Comedy gold. Ken could see humour everywhere and had such a skill with words and an ear for dialect. I was in the audience that night when he regaled us with the whole story and recreated the whole exchange in a brilliant Fife accent. It brought the hall down! Genius.

As the mirthquake died down there was a name being bandied about the hall, obviously the cheeky assistant had form! Ken tried to get on with the show and said "Right, what will we sing?" A wee boy called out to him to sing 'Where's My Shirt'? Ken apologised that his band didn't have the music for that one, then sang it anyway unaccompanied because a child had asked him.

Cont.

A real star, showing his class. Somebody else shouted "Sing yer ain favourite". Ken replied that they would run him out if he did that as it was now a football anthem. It was You'll Never Walk Alone, years before Celtic adopted it as their anthem. He got the go ahead from someone in the wings and again sang unaccompanied but with a large backing choir!

That was really the end of the show, but just before he sang Happiness Ken's parting shot was "I'm getting out of here before you take the carpet up and start dancing"! Magic moments.

Sandra Wallace

Dear Doddy,

I first heard your song Tears when I was very young. When I got to my teens I admired you for your comedy, a world that seemed so wonderful to me. From then I started to collect Variety and Theatre Memorabilia including everything Doddy. In 2011 I saw you for the first time at Southport. The following year I met you backstage at Southport thanks to my now dear friend Veronica Yorke. From then I came to see you twice a year at Southport and I wrote to you and you were so kind to reply every time.

Thanks to you I meet a wide range of wonderful variety friends and my now husband Jimmy Patton who himself and his Brother Brian Patton worked with you back in the 1970's. They are both devastated by today's news of your passing as am I, you where my hero and dear friend. The end of Good Old Fashioned Comedy has gone but I myself and others will keep it alive.

Rest In Peace my Diddy Friend.

All our love

Amy Patton Elliott (Diddy Amy From Ormskirk) & The Patton Brothers (Jimmy & Brian). XxxX

It is the end of an era, one of the all time comics has died. Doddy was loved throughout the UK. I was lucky enough to see his show in Poole and I'm a Liverpool lass and did I laugh, I was aching with laughter. My friend and I got out at 12.40am. Quite early really. I was even tickled by his famous tickling stick in 1966 when Ken was going into Owen Owens.

Cont.

Ken was kind in many ways and in the early 60's when he was playing in pubs, if he saw my Dad waiting for a late night bus home, after finishing his late shift, as a bus conductor, Ken would stop his car and give Dad a lift.

Ken will be missed, a light has gone out forever.

RIP and YNWA

K KING OF COMEDIANS
E ENTERTAINER EXTRAORDINAIRE
N NOMADIC AND NOCTURNAL

D DAUNTLESSLY DEDICATED
O OFFICIALLY O.B.E.D
D DELIGHTFULLY DESCRIPTIVE
D DETERMINED AND DIGINIFIED

Rosemarie Jones

If...

If a stage could whisper, and walls could talk.

If a Theatre could breathe, had eyes of a hawk.

If a tired old venue could make a wish heard.

If an empty dressing room could utter a word.

If bricks and mortar could like magic respond.

If with circles and stalls I could make a bond.

If a Theatre could only listen, and offer a reply.

If only a Venue had its own thoughts to supply.

Imagine that was possible for a second or two.

I bet they all had heroes, just like me and you!

And through the decades of fashion and trend.

Of curtain calls, from shows beginning to end.

That hero would be Doddy, no need for more!

If such things could cry, we'd see tears for sure.

Mike Bartram

10 Little Diddymen

10 little Diddymen, walking in a row.
10 little Diddymen, waiting for a show.
Today I saw them on Blackpool Prom.
Wondering where their Doddy had gone.

10 little Diddymen walking by the sea.
Wondering where their Doddy could be.
10 little Diddymen searching the coast.
'We are the Diddymen' they proudly boast!

10 little Diddymen, they ask passers-by.
'Have you seen our Doddy'? but no reply.
As nobody wanted to break their heart.
10 little Diddymen, a new search to start.

10 little Diddymen, walking on the beach
'Why is our beloved Doddy out of reach!?
Diddy footprints barely disturbed the sand.
10 little Diddymen, a new search planned.

10 little Diddymen, footprints on the shore.
10 little Diddymen at the Grand stage door.
Asking the same question time after time.
'Where's our Doddy' just give us a sign?

10 little Diddymen now Knotty Ash bound.
In Blackpool their Doddy couldn't be found.
And I feel so hearbroken for all of them.
Doddy's lost and lonely, 10 little Diddymen.

10 little Diddymen, now I see them all cry.
And I think I know the tragic reason why.
But Doddy's just in Heaven, so cry no more.
Still be happy with your memories galore!

Mike Bartram

Last year I travelled from Australia to England and was delighted and privileged to see Ken's show in St Helens, on 5 October - he never missed a beat. My condolences to his family at this sad time.

Lyndon Crabbe, Perth, Australia.

Please can we offer our sincere condolences to our dear friend on the loss of Ken. He was a good friend a very warm and kind and caring gentleman.

From Veronica & David Yorke and family +Ann from Salford

God bless you Ken, you were an inspiration to everyone, part of my childhood, teenage & also later yrs also. You will be missed. Your unending wit, tickling stick, of course, great singing voice & those diddymen by jove, we loved so much too!

Tattybye Ken, tattybye & RIP!

Like Laurel & Hardy, Ken was not only very very funny, but even as a child, you could tell he was a Nice and genuine person. I cherish the times I saw him and I don't think I've ever laughed so much and for so long. It's the end of an era and the UK will be a sadder place without him but Thankful we had him around for a long time. R.I.P Ken, You were the Best.

Ian, Sydney

Cont.

48

I am so very sorry to hear of your passing. I always knew this day would come at some point, and I knew that I would heartbroken when it did, and I am. I remember watching you on TV when I was younger, and I couldn't stop laughing - I loved your silly yet creative humour, and I loved your positive approach to life. I went to see you twice at The Stockport Plaza with my Mum, and we had the best time (and a long time....!)

I had said to my Mum that we really needed to see you again before you left us - but unfortunately that wasn't to be.....you needed to leave us to make heaven laugh.

We will miss you, but we will remember you always.

Tatty Bye Ken!

Love Zoe

X

The Squire of Knotty Ash

Up in Heaven God and the Angels await.

For Doddy's arrival at St Peters gate.

Doddy's been called, it was simply his time.

He worked so hard for every laughter line.

In his beloved Knotty Ash, tears they fell.

To the sound of a passing, mourning bell.

The flags of the City hung at half mast.

As Doddy joined the elite of Heavens cast.

A unique entertainer, and one of our own.

In Knotty Ash he always felt most at home.

He was a 'man of the people' undeniably so.

Always gave his time with a cheery 'hello'

Now, I can picture the applause, the cheer.

And the laughter of Angels I can almost hear.

As Sir Ken plays a new stage way up high.

To the Squire of Knotty Ash, we say 'Goodbye'

Mike Bartram

Waking up to hear that the great Ken Dodd had died filled me with much sadness, me and my grandad when he was alive would sit and watch his videos over and over again, we'd always laugh at the same jokes even though we'd heard them many times before, sadly I'm from sunny Essex and cannot make it to Liverpool to say goodbye to a legend, thank you for bringing the world so much happiness Sir Ken, you've left a void that no one will fill, there's simply no one around who did what you did, how will milkman cope without the extra pay from all the lifts home they've have to give all your patrons who missed there last route home.

RIP Sir Kenneth Arthur Dodd one in a million!

Richard Davies

In memory of a great, funny and wonderfully musical man. Will be missed by all and remembered as the greatest talented man that he was. RIP Ken, making them laugh in heaven xx

Carol Pennell

As a teenager, in London, I was passionately in love with Ken. Whereas all the other girls at school were mad about McCartney, Lennon and Jagger for me it was Ken and the cause of much ridicule and bullying by my peers. I left school at 15 to look after my invalid mother. I would write to Ken regularly and he would send me tickets to all his radio and television shows.

I got to know him really well. One night I missed the last tube train back to Brixton from Shepherd's Bush and went running

Cont.

5 1

back to the theatre in the hope that someone might give me a lift at least part way. When no-one offered Ken was really annoyed as he knew one couple could have diverted. He said, "I'm not having this!" and went to speak to his taxi driver, who radioed me a cab. Ken refused to leave, even though he'd a train to catch, until I was safely in my taxi and gave me £2 for my fare home. I never forgot his many kindnesses to me and over the years have always held him in the greatest affection and esteem.

My heart goes out to his family, especially Lady Anne, at this sad time. The wonderful thing is we know that Ken is now in Glory with the Lord he loved, and although we mourn his departure from this life we have the promise to meet again if we too trust in Jesus.

Christine Normington

Final Curtain

Wonderful stories we all have to share and tell.

If people knew Doddy, they simply loved him as well!

Loving, sincere tributes to Doddy, page after page.

And how are people remembered, love is the gauge!

With Doddy and his Diddymen in Knotty Ash I grew.

Something's now not right, do you feel that way too?

The greatest entertainer the world has ever known.

As I pass his house, I can't believe he's not at home.

The legend that is Doddy, is safe for ever and a day.

He was a timeless genius, no barriers stood in his way.

The admiration of his fans will be impossible to quell.

He'll live on forever, long after his final curtain has fell.

Mike Bartram

The Happiness Show

The months fly by, already passed have three.

A summer season without our Doddy to see.

No Blackpool show in the shadow of the Tower.

No Doddy shows running late, hour after hour!

No more waiting for our hero at the stage door.

Treated to a mammoth show, 4 hours or more!

Doddy never allowed his act to become stale.

Old and new material combined, he couldn't fail!

Up and coming shows displayed on a venues list.

One name more than any other so sorely missed.

Sadly missing is The Ken Dodd Happiness Show.

With its endless roaring laughter from every row!

Mike Bartram

John Hulse & Adam Croft top/below John Hulse

KEN DODD

Knotty Ash
Liverpool L14 5NX

Dear Harrington Family

Some time ago you very kindly wrote to me to say how
much you had enjoyed the show. I was delighted to
hear from you and very much appreciated your good
wishes and kind remarks.

I am very sorry for this long delay in replying to you;
unfortunately your letter was mislaid for a while and
has only just come to light with some other correspondence.

Thank you, once again, for taking the trouble to write
to me.

Kind regards,

Yours sincerely,

Ken Dodd

⭑ enclosed show list as requested.

Courtesy Michael Harrington

Rosemarie Jones

Drawing by Ken 2000 courtesy Rosemarie Jones

Joe Brady

Sam Jephcote

This was Summer Season 1981 Southport we were a girl dance act called Hot Spice... Ken saw us in Bridlington when we were doing a split week with him he stayed over watched the show and offered us the job! His wife Annie was in the show with us she was a country and western singer! Little bit of history there for you! After this we then added to the group had a name change to Sweet Spice and did Nottingham, The London Palladium and then went to Blackpool to the Opera House for summer season 1981! Happy days.

Fran Sheppard

How many of the other comedians could tour the country with in effect the same show year after year and get a full house every time. And all without being on the latest talk shows to promote it.

They all know Ken was the best and not one of them could come close.

Helen McIntyre

We loved Ken. He's been there all our lives making us and our parents laugh. We saw him at Birmingham Hippodrome about 15 years ago. We left in the pouring rain at 1.20 am! Wonderful comedian and very nice person.

Gillian Gallet

Cont.

Judging by the Liverpool comedians who turned up to pay their respects to Ken at his funeral and what they had to say about him, they worshipped him as much as we '"friends of Ken's" do.

Peter Lewis

They did Peter. Listening to their tributes I was nodding along thinking he's said that to me when we met etc, which shows what a truly remarkable man Ken was. He treated everyone the same famous or not. He loved people and was always interested in you as a person regardless of who you were or where you were from.

Helen McIntyre.

Ken never had to use filth, he didn't need to, and his performances were absolutely his and his alone, no copying other people, just straight forward KEN DODD.

Roy Beswick

The endearing aspects of Ken's character certainly shone through and enhanced our love of the man as the top comedian of the day, which put him a league of his own in more ways than one!

Peter Lewis

For Sir Kenneth Dodd

A day after Mother's Day
we heard of your death.
Kenny.
Canny.
Funny for so many,
you were mother to my humour
and father to my mood.
Laughed like I've never laughed before;
saw you live; so wished it had been more.
You were on my Bucket List.
Learnt so much about the art of funny,
I raved about these long long shows:
what you could learn from them,
what had me in gales of laughter
in the harbour of audience.
The plank jokes and the Wake-Up Drum.
The singing and the music hall.
'A Jester', you said, you wanted
to be remembered as.
I saw how what you did-
a ventriloquism of a special kind
deft yet see-through, I lapped it up.
You worked us like puppets;
The great Suggester.
Same house for ninety years.
A home of comedy and of privacy

Cont.

As I age and I get dafter
and death and taxes come to take a bow
It's good to know that even after
the long show is over
these things are now
beyond our Ken.

Ruth Chalkley

It is impossible to forget or disregard the love and laughter, time and patience you shared with us all so effortlessly. You will always remain in our minds and hearts a gentle jester and I shall personally carry you with me all the remaining days of my life. It was an honour to shake your hand and stand in your light.

Amanda J Morris (AJ) – Sender of Sweat Peas

Rest in Peace, Sir Ken Dodd, sing with the Angels your voice is beautiful.

Helen Hart, Withernsea, East Riding of Yorkshire

Rest in peace Ken. We will miss you so very, very much. You were not one of the best you were the best. Beautiful memories.

Ron, Irene Marston Stourbridge West Midlands

Many thanks Ken for allowing me to exercise my chuckle muscles on many occasions, you have given years of selfless service now it's time to rest

Rest in peace....in between making the angels laugh xxx

Barbara Tomlinson

It was a privilege to have met such a kind, caring gentleman who brought so much happiness to so many people. The memories I have of your shows and of meeting you, I will cherish forever. Thoughts are with Lady Anne and families.

Helen McIntyre

Cont.

The world is a much darker and more solemn place now that the light of one of its' greatest ever comic geniuses has gone out. Rest in peace Sir Ken. Such treasured memories of hours of joyous laughter, hypnotised by your effortless, unstinting and unmatchable skill of making people laugh. We shall think of you often.

Paul, Karen and Lewis Woods xxx (Cardiff)

Thank you Ken for all the laughter you have given us over the years. I am now nearly 60 and have very fond memories as a child watching you and the diddy men. Loving your shows over the years and finally managing to see you at the civic hall in Wolverhampton in one of your final performances. I stayed to the very end, which was well past my bedtime, and loved every minute of it. A true legend. God bless.

Brian Hulse

Knotty Ash

Does Knotty Ash really exist I hear, well let me take you there.
On Thomas Lane there's a nursery, for little children they care.
Close by is St Johns Church, that's where Doddy used to pray.
Around the corner the playing fields, on football I used to play.

On Brookside Avenue is the house I lived, just in the square.
The happiest memories years of my life, I have got from there.
But when love finally ran its course, it was time to move away.
And I will truly regret that ever happened, until my dying day.

Where *are* the Jam Butty Mines, to find them use your head!
Use your imagination to discover them, not just an A to Z!
The same goes for those gravy trains, Knotty Ash gravy on tap.
We have Doddy to thank for such things, to put us on the map.

Then of course there's Doddy's house, a life he lived there whole.
That's where he took on the title, the 'Squire of Knotty Ash' role.
Today I see beautiful flowers and tributes, each side of the gate.
As God wanted an audience with Doddy, and could no longer wait.

And how did 'Knotty Ash' get its name, simple answer from a tree!
It was a knotted and gnarled Ash, a landmark for travellers to see.
I love Knotty Ash, and so lucky to bump into Doddy many times.
And like Doddy proudly said, it's even got its own Motorway signs!

Mike Bartram

Fan's Tribute

The last time I saw Ken was when I went to see his show at the Blackpool Grand on the 22nd of October 2017 for my 18th birthday. I had written to tell him it was my birthday and Lady Anne recognised me in the queue and gave me a programme and a present from the merchandise table. Then it was show time I was on the front row and I've never seen a show that's funnier I've watched him many times but this was by far the best he had ever performed it he was so happy and full of energy because Blackpool was throwing a celebration the same day for his 90th birthday!

So the show went on and towards the end when the show starts to get more emotional and Doddy thanks the audience and speaks to the audience he started thanking the Mayor and Mayoress for coming along to the show and when he did the 'party list' he also mentioned my name - "now we have a young comedian in the audience Joe Brady and he has told me before how keen he is to become a comedian and I have given him some advice and encouragement –   all the best Joe wishing you success and happiness in your chosen career and also Happy Birthday" At this point I was looking at my Dad and we thought my God Ken Dodd my hero is talking about me on stage to all of these people it can't get any better than this can it.

At the end of the show I waited outside the stage door with several other people and he spoke to each and every one of us., It was getting quite late but he had time for everybody and when he got round to me Ken asked me what I was doing with my comedy and what I was going to do, and he gave me advice, material and just general life lessons.

Cont.

It was an absolute master class about comedy but more importantly it was just having a chat with a friend. He arranged with the Manager Shaun to let me go on the stage! (at the Blackpool Grand which he knew was my favourite theatre a dream come true!!) I had never been happier than I was that night - no one on this planet has or will ever have a better 18th than me you can't beat that can you?

And then as they were driving off the last thing he ever said to me he shouted out the window of his Mercedes "Joe, I promise I'm not on pills!!". I made a promise to Ken that night that I would spend my life spreading happiness to people through entertainment like he did, and he believed I could and would. I could not thank Ken or Anne enough for the happiness, and the advice they gave me but most importantly for their time and their friendship as it meant and does mean so much to me. I will forever miss Ken but I will keep my promise to him, because I said so. Happiness always.

Joe Brady

Doddy Poem

As the raindrops fell on knotty ash
A sad silence did descend
The Diddymen could laugh no more
They had lost their greatest friend

The treacle and Jam Butty Mines
Under Dicky Mint's instruction
Decided it was only right
To immediately stop production

The broken Biscuit repair works
Repaired biscuits by the score
But they couldn't fix a broken heart
Of that they now were sure

The Snuff Quarries and the Moggy Ranch
They too were in despair
They searched around for Happiness
But alas... there was non there.

Such sadness over Liverpool
Where once there was great fun
Such grey and damp and drizzle
Where once there was the sun

Cont.

Alone they sat in silence
Animated by their grief
Sid Short and Smarty Arty
Struck dumb.... in disbelief

Then Nicky Nugget....without warning
Stood up and shouted 'Quick!!'
And reaching down behind the couch
He grabbed a tickling stick

'By Jove!' He shrieked... we mustn't weep
That doesn't help nobody
For as long as we have laughter
We will always have our Doddy

Mike & Judith Sands Vera Andalusia Spain.

A fan's letter to Lady Anne

Please forgive the intrusion at this sad time but I felt uncharacteristically compelled to write a personal note of condolence to add to the legions of sentiments expressed by other fans right now.

Now in my early 60s I've been a lifelong fan of Sir Ken – ever since I met him when on holiday with two friends as teenagers in Scarborough after a show there in the early 70s.

Ken was surprised to meet three young lads at the stage door after midnight– he must have been exhausted but still welcomed us back in to have a chat, share a great gag (about Scarborough girls!) as well as a beer and gave us signed postcards and free tickets to a forthcoming show.

A wonderful moment none of us (we're still great friends) have ever forgotten.

I've seen his live show at least five times (modest by super fan standards, I know) and know all (well virtually all, still surprised occasionally by a new one) his quips & gags and repeat them to friends and family incessantly ... "as Ken Dodd says..." a daily mantra.

I love all things comedic but he really was the only comic who never failed to make me laugh out loud. Always.

Now a regular contributor to the 'Friends of Sir Ken' Facebook site I, like many others thought he was just brilliant. Loved him. His passing is somehow like a family member going and the world is a less happy place now but I'll do my best to keep his memory – and his gags – alive, at least in my family!

Cont.

My wife, also a fan of course and I last saw you & Ken perform live in Watford May 2016 -a 60th birthday present whence after another 5 hr brilliant show I captured two tickling sticks that have pride of place now in my study.

Words cannot express the sorrow you must be experiencing right now after so long together – only perhaps alleviated by the tide of love and emotion that Sir Ken's peers and adoring fans are now expressing.

He was unique and will be sorely missed but what joy he brought to the world.

My heartfelt sympathies to you. Stay strong.

Yours truly

John Wringe

My endearing memory of Doddy was in the 60s when I was about 10. My Mum was going to a dinner at the top rank with Doddy as special guest. It was after one of his shows and she was going to take me too. I had on my Sunday best dress and when we got there I wasn't allowed in. I burst in to tears as I had been wanting to see him. He came out to talk to me and gave me his autograph. I still have it.

Patricia Corlett

It is nice to see so many posts every day on Sir Ken's site, reading all the many memories that people have of him. I can always remember my Mum and Dad had his LP "Hits For Now And Always", (they didn't have many records but this was one of them) and growing up in the 70's we had one of those old large gramophone record cabinets, with the radio at one side and record player at the other and this record was played a lot over the years, and my all-time favourite song "The River" is on it. I have been a fan ever since. I still have the record to this day, plus many others.

John Higton

Words we always heard said about Ken in both life and sadly in his passing were...He was "the comedian's comedian". Whilst other comedy stars may have topped various polls or been flavour of the moment. On the circuit and among his contemporaries and peers, Doddy was regarded as the best of them all.

Mark Wakeman

Cont.

He was a patron of our Theatre and I was Stage Manager for him for several years when he came to play us. A real Gent, a pleasure to work with but a real nightmare to get to go home. His audiences might have thought that they'd had a long night but we were usually several hours later. On one occasion, whilst he was chatting to the crew at 3:45am, Annie grabbed him by the arm and said "We are going home whether you want to or not!"

Roy, Crew Plaza

Top fella, best I've seen

John Roach

I was in Blackpool just before Easter and popped into The Grand Theatre, they had Ken's photo on the booking desk with some white roses, I wanted to sign condolence book but it had already been sent to the family. I've got lots of memories of seeing Ken in Blackpool.

Denise Best x

Doddy Poem

Wish I could see you one more time,
to hear the beautiful songs you would sing.
To listen to your crazy jokes ,
and share the joy you would bring.

Wish I could be in a theatre once more,
laughing till my sides ache.
Instead I sit here with nowhere to go,
and my heart trying hard not to break.

Wish I could wait at the stage door one more time,
no matter how wet or how cold.
To shake your hand and talk some more,
and share wonderful memories of old.

You bought me joy when I was in pain,
and turned bad times into good.
And you eased my sorrows with laughter,
in a way that only you could.

Now just one thing makes me feel a little less sad
for deep in my heart I know.
That up there you're now doing a heavenly show.
and in the audience, are my late mum and dad!

Elaine R Jones

A very humble man. He once said it didn't matter what you do in life but never forget who put you where you are. He also said always look them in the eyes and always be sincere. The best advice I was ever given.

Sean Hornby

Around 1957/8 I was 15 and Ken 30, I spotted him crossing Lime Street, Liverpool towards the Royal Court Theatre. I approached him with my trusty trendy autograph book and asked him for his autograph, on opening the book he spotted an Everton players signature and said tongue in cheek "You don't expect me to sign next to him do you?" he did of course. No malice with Ken.

John Grant

I was lucky to have seen Ken each year in Blackpool when I was a little girl, it was the highlight of our holiday.

Denise Best

Someone asked me why was Ken Dodd so special apart from the fact that he never used any bad language? My Reply was instant...

Because his humour came from everyday life, never a day goes by without me saying something Ken said, and I laugh, and that day was brighter straight away. So not only did he make us laugh at the shows but in between as well, and that is why he is so very special to me.

Cont.

What amazing value for money his shows lasted all year not just for one night.

Rosemarie Jones

As a member of an NHS Choir I would go every year, along with other choirs from the North West, to the North West NHS Christmas Carol Service at the Anglican Cathedral in Liverpool. Every year Ken would attend the service and give a speech. Christmas 2017 we sang Happiness for him waving tickling sticks.

We will really miss him coming to our Christmas Concerts, it won't feel the same this Christmas. God Bless you Ken.

Kim Prince

We need humour in our lives and By Jove he left us with some wonderful one-liners. We must be grateful that we have DVD's and CD's of him. We were lucky in that we lived when he did. Marvelous man.

Dorothy Kazer

...Doddy His Name

The London Palladium '65, top of the bill.

A forty two week house run, a record still!

Forty two great weeks, on top of his game.

The funniest man ever...Doddy his name!

Forty two weeks of no stop fun and cheer.

Rapid fire jokes and songs for all to hear.

Tears of laughter will have fallen like rain.

The funniest man ever...Doddy his name!

A ventriloquist act, a little tongue in cheek!

No tricky lines did Dicky Mint have to speak!

He had in me stiches, my sides sore in pain.

The funniest man ever...Doddy his name!

Now we miss our Doddy on stage and TV,

The greatest entertainer you will ever see.

But I suppose our loss is now Heavens gain.

The funniest man ever, 'Sir Doddy' his name.

Mike Bartram

Ken Dodd was the greatest entertainer I ever saw, the greatest comedian, certainly, but he was so much more. He did the joy, he did the sorrow, he sung such lovely songs. He touched the human chord deep within us all. I could give any number of reasons why he was the greatest as such, but his talent, like love, has no need of proof. You just needed to see him in his natural habitat, among the people, and you would know. He was the people's comedian.

Words cannot really express my love and admiration for a man who moved so many with joy and laughter for so long. It is so sad to think that this man who could give so much joy and laughter will never be seen again, but there is great thanks for the immense happiness he brought to the world. Ken Dodd was a one-off, and we were truly blessed to be part of his charmed circle.

I'm thinking of absent friends in my own family, going back to grandparents, aunties, my mother, all of whom he had aching with laughter, tears rolling down their cheeks.

'But it's what I love to do,' Ken said modestly. I'll say it from him: Ken Dodd was the very best at what he loved to do. He was the best of his kind, and his kind is the best.

"I won't hang my tickling stick up until I have to."

Every road must end, even Doddy's, and only death could persuade Doddy to put his tickling stick down and leave his beloved stage. Come 12-30am tonight, I'll be thinking of Doddy and raising a glass to the man who brought so much happiness to the world.

Tatty bye, dear Ken, our very absent, ever present, friend for always.

Smiling Angels

I believe in Heaven jokes are being told.

Tears down the face of Angels have rolled.

Do 'late nights' in Heaven I wonder exist?

As one more story Doddy couldn't resist!

And to 'absent friends' Ken has said 'hello'

And still playing the best ever 1 man show.

I guess God wanted to laugh with Doddy too.

So for us mortals, memories will have to do.

By Jove with what memories we are blessed!

As the Squire has earned his heavenly rest.

The greatest entertainer ever had to depart.

But Ken Dodd will always live on in our heart.

Mike Bartram

My husband and I were lucky enough to see him at the Echo Arena in December 2017, he was an absolutely funny man, no swearing etc in his jokes just daft and funny. An honour and privilege to see you. RIP Sir Ken

When I was working in the Dovecot Mac with the previously named Liverpool JET Service, (Jobs Education & Training, now known as Liverpool In Work) Sir Ken paid us a visit. What an honour.

He asked me if I could get him a job as a Gigolo. I told him that I thought he was over qualified for that job, and why didn't he consider hairdressing instead. He laughed out loudly and agreed that was a better choice, and proceeded to ruffle his hair. Smiles and laughter all around.

A lovely, lovely man, one of Liverpool's finest, a city he loved, and a true comic genius, the like of which will never be seen again.

R.I.P Sir Ken. Liverpool will have many "Tears for Souvenirs" The legend will live on...

Cathy Clements

It was Sunday 20th August 2017 at Whitley Bay. I've been to three shows but this was the one! It was an early start of 5pm, the show finished at 10:30pm and as we left the theatre to the sound of happiness I waited outside beside the stage door, it was very chilly. The clock ticked and ticked and by now I was getting very nervous about meeting my hero.

It was getting late but still I waited in disbelief I was going to meet Ken Dodd! Then the door opened wide Lady Anne waved us all in, I walked in and there he stood with a beautiful smile. I of course froze in the spot and was lost for words. I walked closer to him and Ken held his hand out for mine, kissed his hand and simply said "beautiful".

I told him he was my hero and how much I loved his show he then said "I'm just a comedian but makes me so happy to know that". He was ever so humble.

He talks to his fans as if we had been friends for years. He was such a gentleman full of compliments but also the joker as he told me I should work in a fire station with such red hair. As we were leaving he said "Good night gorgeous". As we drove away he waved and smiled.

Jade Melissa

Sir Ken, I want to thank you for all the special messages for over 45 years in your Christmas cards signed always including Lady Anne. I'm so Tickled to have so many memories which will live forever in my heart. Sir Ken, you always treated everyone like family, had a kind word to say to everyone you met. Tatty-Bye For Now dear friend.

Pamela & Jim Schuler

California U.S. A.

Words

Up in Heaven, Doddy has some words to share.

In life there was no time for them to prepare.

Because God was in a hurry, for Doddy no pain.

Time to marry his bride, a beautiful wife to gain.

Aptly his final concert, a sell out Liverpool show.

Sadly, a little time later it was Dodddy's time to go.

No more classic Doddy, story, joke song or pun.

The world had lost its King of laughter mirth and fun.

Those words from Doddy, *can* now see the light.

'Thank you my fans, God bless you and goodnight'

Mike Bartram

A Born Comic

Once again up in Heaven they applaud.

A show for the Angels one for The Lord.

You just can't keep a born comic down!

The greatest entertainer ever to hit Town!

In Heaven Ken Dodd's star shines bright.

All the other stars they blink at the sight.

Heaven of course is such a restful place.

No clocks to watch and no time to race.

That suits our Doddy down to the ground.

Recall his late shows, no buses to be found!

But hey Doddy, now catch up on your sleep.

In Heaven, no rush, all your jokes will keep!

And when you find a spare moment or two.

Please look at our book we have wrote for you!

Mike Bartram

Kerry

Helen McIntyre

Sandra Borgazzi

Shaun Gorringe

Samuel Ball

John Martin

John Devonport

David Gregson

Brian Fisher top/below Tom Fisher

Jade Melissa

SIR KEN DODD OBE   Knotty Ash, January 2017

Dear Dave

I am writing to thank you most sincerely for your good wishes and
congratulations on the knighthood recently bestowed upon me.
Your friendship and kind words are much appreciated and it is good to hear
that you are happy for me.

I am grateful for all the wonderful and joyous occasions I have had
in my life. The messages of affection and goodwill that I have received from
all over of the country mean so much to me.
I feel blessed that I have been able to enjoy entertaining British audiences for
many years. Thank you again.

Friends are our treasure, they are more precious than gold.
I wish you a New Year full of Happiness!
Kindest regards from me, as I will always be

Thank you for all the memories!

Ken

Courtesy David Gregson

Rick Minns (Ruddy Muddy)

Comedy legend's always been tonic

BLACKPOOL favourite Ken Dodd is back in the resort this weekend for the first of his now-legendary run of Illuminations Sunday night shows at the Grand Theatre.

His season lasts until October 28 and the theatre website even carries a "warning" that the performance by the mirthmaker – who is 80 in November – lasts approximately five hours!

That means a lot of belly laughs and fans would suggest Ken's act is such a tonic that it should be available to all on the NHS.

Colleagues

And, as this picture shows, 40 years ago the Knotty Ash funnyman was indeed dispensing his unique brand of laughter medicine across the wards – and across the airwaves.

Seen with him is David Gregson, a pioneer of Blackpool Radio Victoria, who says: "The service was first on air on August 10, 1967, developed from my idea, having had help from my colleagues Jean Goodrick and Brian Henderson.

"The station was built by my late father Frank Greg-

JUST WHAT THE DOCTOR ORDERED: Ken Dodd with Radio Victoria pioneer David Gregson in 1967 at the launch of the station

son over many weeks in the bowels of the hospital.

"All the family were involved at one time or another in the early days of the station and I also did patient interviews and outside broadcasts with help from Post Office telephones (Now BT)."

And so to Ken Dodd's involvement.

David says: "I worked backstage at the time in the Opera House and did lots of star interviews for the station with people like Val

Doonican, Millicent Martin, Bruce Forsyth, Tessie O' Shea to name but a few.

"When the station started it was known as Blackpool Hospitals Broadcasting Service and was opened by Ken Dodd who was appearing for a summer season at the Blackpool Opera House.

"I was delighted when he agreed to be the very first guest and with me also interviewing him as well!

"Looking back at the time that I spent as a radio pre-

senter for the hospital service I really enjoyed making a difference to the patients.

"On odd occasions we even went up to the wards to say hello.

"All of the staff that worked on the radio show were volunteers who, like myself, just wanted to give something back to the community."

■ See Monday's Gazette for a review of the star's show at the Grand

Blackpool Gazette 1967

John Martin

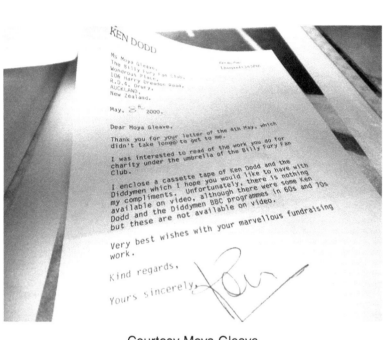

KEN DODD

Ms Moya Gleave,
The Billy Fury Fan Club,
Wondrous Place,
106 Harry Dreanon Road,
R.D.4, Drury,
AUCKLAND,
New Zealand.

May, 8th 2000.

Dear Moya Gleave,

Thank you for your letter of the 4th May, which
didn't take long@ to get to me.

I was interested to read of the work you do for
charity under the umbrella of the Billy Fury Fan
Club.

I enclose a cassette tape of Ken Dodd and the
Diddymen which I hope you would like to have with
my compliments. Unfortunately, there is nothing
available on video, although there were some Ken
Dodd and the Diddymen BBC programmes in 60s and 70s
but these are not available on video.

Very best wishes with your marvellous fundraising
work.

Kind regards,

Yours sincerely,

Courtesy Moya Gleave

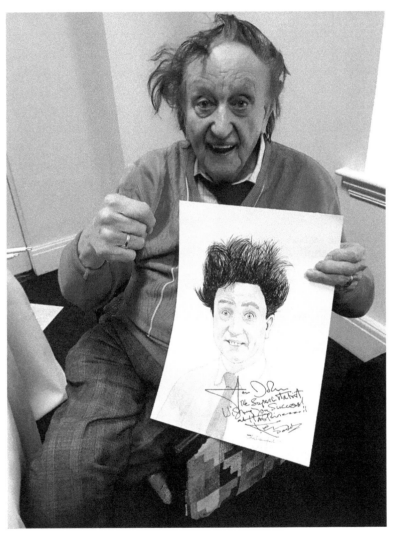

Ken with John Devonport portrait

Fan's Tribute

It was April, 2000 when my sister and I went to Poland. It was to visit our late father who is laid to rest there. We stayed in Krakow and whilst we were there we decided to visit Auschwitz so we organised a trip by our hotel. On the day of our trip we got on a coach and along the way it picked up other people, at a big hotel a couple got on which were Ken and Anne, Ken was wearing his signature checked coat and they sat right behind us. We couldn't believe it was him at first but after introductions we just started talking, he was very nice and just ordinary and wanted to know why we were there etc...

When we got to Auschwitz, Ken and Anne were in our party and we walked around together. Myself and Ken got on well and I linked him as we chatted and looked at things, my sister and Anne following behind, Anne was taking a video of the place. It was quite surreal to be with a comedian in such a sorrowful place but it was like we had known each other for a long time. Whilst we were there and looking at the exhibitions of which one was one of suitcases behind glass, on the suitcases people had wrote their details as they had thought they were going to a holiday camp not a death one.

We also stood in front of the scaffold of where the commandant of the camp was hung, it was eerie as we both noticed on looking at the notice plaque it was that day the 16th of April. There were lots of other aspects and it became aware Ken was a very emotional, humble and reverent soul as well as being such a funny man.

Cont.

Then as we left, we had some pictures took with him, which I have somewhere and that's when he made my sister and I Diddy ladies. He placed his hands on our shoulders and gracefully named us, we felt quite special. We went back on the coach and said our goodbyes as they got off before us. We'll never forget that day or beloved Ken x

Juliana Campbell

Diddyladies (For Juliana and Vera !)

The Diddymen are famous, we see them every day.

But what about 'Diddyladies' I hear people often say.

In these days of equality, it's only right and fair.

'Diddyladies' too exist, complete with funny hair!

But what I surprise I got today and so little did I know.

That Diddyladies *already* exist, a message told me so!

One day a few years ago Doddy bestowed that fame.

When to a lady he gave that honour, Juliana her name!

She may not have the funny teeth, or wear a funny hat.

But she's *still* a 'Diddylady' Doddy himself saw to that!

Mike Bartram

Raised Bar

I think of what Doddy achieved in his day.

All other comedians he simply blew away.

But in doing that, in being ahead so far.

He understandably raised the comedy bar!

But he raised it to such a ridiculous height.

All competitors where beaten out of sight!

A height that others couldn't hope to leap.

So the comedy crown will be Ken's to keep!

A little unfair on other comics it may seem.

To fill Doddy's boots is an impossible dream.

All truthful comedians would admit that too.

As they admired Doddy, just as his fans do.

Being Liverpool born, gave Ken a head start.

A genuine funny person, with a massive heart.

His hilarious act performed in a unique style.

He raised that comedy bar by a country mile!

Mike Bartram

Doddy, My Mum and Dad are in heaven laughing with you now I'm sure! They just loved you and saw you on stage many, many times.......Mum fell asleep in 2007 and took with her 'her tickling stick' that she had been fortunate to catch at one of your shows......my Dad left our sight last July ....as a 'homage' to both of them my husband and I came to your show in Llandudno last August. I am so happy we did we were not disappointed and would have seen you again in January but it wasn't to be...fond memories live on.

Our thoughts and prayers are with Lady Anne and your family, you will never be forgotten......in time the tears will lessen and the happiness you brought will shine through again........

Let's raise a glass to absent friends.

May you Rest In Peace Ken with your Diddy Men Love From Sharon

I am saddened by the news of Ken Dodd and I shall remember all the many hours of laughter he gave me as a young child with my dad. That was the start continuing throughout my life there will be never anyone to replace him as he has left a legacy of material though he's not with us he will always be with us

RIP Charles Oakes Bolton

Cont.

In memory of a superb comedian and gentleman who had the God-given ability to make people laugh and is still as popular today as he was when he first started in "the business". We were fortunate to have him for so long. Gone, but never forgotten.

R.I.P. Ken and deepest sympathy to his wife, Lady Anne. Rita Leyland

Dear Ken you will be missed by all. You were a true entertainer and comic genius. Thank you for honouring my mum Hilda Fallon I'm certain she is playing her piano for you and you are singing in heaven. RIP Ken from Jill Robinson daughter of Hilda Fallon xx

A life lived to the full and so much happiness given to so many people all over the world. We are so grateful we had the opportunity to see him on many occasions, Ken will live on, and he was the Greatest.

From Pam and Roger in Llandudno

A Letter to Heaven

I'm sorry Doddy, I hope for now just my poem will do.

I never sent you a letter, though I was always meaning to.

That poem just came to me, in the early hours of night.

Letting go of hands is hard, especially when held so tight.

'Never put off till tomorrow'... I recall your advice so wise.

Now tomorrow will never come, no time for 'goodbyes'

A letter to you I could still write and put it in Heavens post.

I'll address it to the comic the whole world loves the most!

But for now Doddy, I hope my little poem you have seen.

It was written in your honour, I called it 'Dicky Mint's Dream'

Mike Bartram

DICKY MINT'S DREAM.

Dicky had a dream, one night. He and Doddy were walking down Blackpool Prom in downs early light.

Looking back he saw Doddys' footprints in the sand as he was held in Doddys' right hand.

Suddenly they were no more.
Only 2 Diddy footprints were left upon the shore.

Dicky cried "DODDY where are you my friend"?!
Doddy replied...

..'I'm sorry Little Man our journey had to end. (You see the Good Lord has called me home).
A journey I must take alone.

Amanda.L. Lewis-Jones

Respect

There something special about Doddys' fan base.

A kind of unique bond amongst fans I see in place.

Described as a 'kindred spirit' on a Facebook page.

Most Doddy fans seem to connect, whatever age!

That's because Doddy to all generations appealed.

A common theme appears in our stories revealed.

Respect *and* appreciation is that common theme.

The Squire and his audience, one huge happy team!

Happy to chat, be it on the street or a stage door.

Does a similar bond exist elsewhere, I'm not so sure?

In this instant World of throwaway success and fame.

Audience appreciation seems to be on the wane.

I've discovered when fans dip into the memory well.

For all their lovely memories and stories to tell.

I know by now what I'll hear and what to expect.

That Doddy treated his fans with the utmost respect.

Mike Bartram

Heavenly Path

It seems odd that since a person has passed away.

I have found myself to be laughing nearly every day!

But then I think to myself, when all said and done.

What better way to remember this lovely man of fun!

And what a magnificent legacy Doddy left behind.

The last of the greats has sadly left us you will find.

He was the greatest comic the world will ever know.

Always modest and humble, never an ego on show.

So I *don't* feel guilty as today once again I laugh.

As our hero Doddy now treads a new Heavenly path.

Mike Bartram

Who is It?

He made people laugh with nothing to say!

With his sticky up hair like a fountain spray.

With verse of song he could make people cry.

The king of entertainment, the reason why!

And when the jokes came, fired thick and fast.

Long into the night, his brilliant act could last.

Part of his act, he was a funny ventriloquist too.

With his best mate, part of his Knotty Ash crew.

A generous man, a true gentleman off stage.

He could make you laugh, whatever your age!

I've not told you his name, but he was unique.

You'll know who I mean without clues to seek!

Mike Bartram

A Man of Many Parts

Doddy make me cry with laughter, which I don't often do!
I laughed at Ken's tittilating stories, saucy but never blue!
As Doddy *never* caused offence, a line he never crossed.
And in conversation with intellects, Ken Dodd was never lost.

Never afraid to laugh at himself, the famous teeth and hair.
Everything he tried his hand at, he had that certain flair.
Stand-up comedian, ventriloquist, singer... take your choice.
And when it comes to singing, he boasted a fantastic voice.

Doddy could play it straight, he played a Twelfth Night part.
Above all I loved his humour, which he'd turned into an art.
I love how he spoke at length about his beloved Knotty Ash.
He was always down to Earth, never a boastful man or brash.

When Doddy topped The Palladium, with his show quick fire.
London was blown away, by our very own Knotty Ash Squire.
He played to packed houses to the end, never an empty seat.
Even when in later ill health, Ken Dodd never accepted defeat!

Doddy was a generous, charitable man, of elegance and style.
I'll always cherish the memory when he spoke to me for a while.
If for the 'most popular scouser ever' they ever conduct a poll.
I will cast my vote for 'The Guvnor' with all my heart and soul.

Mike Bartram

There are no good comedians now in my opinion, Sir Ken was the last and was someone you would pay to see, and know you'd get your money's worth, without insults or offending anyone or resorting to filth or bad language, he had the audience in the palm of his hand, a quite brilliant and funny man who leaves me in stitches even though he's no longer with us, legend is an overused word but this great man was a legend.

Stewart Sherwin

I would describe it as "Ken had an instinctive and unique God-given understanding of how comedy worked and carried on a love affair with us his audience.

Peter Lewis

Ken knew his audience he will remain the best entertainer of all time, and the proudest credit to Doddy he could have you laughing without anything blue no swearing a bit saucy but nothing that you couldn't tell your grandmother / or any member of the family a genuine man all round from singing and his comedy there will never be another like Doddy, 'by Jove Missus' what a fine day and bless you Lady Doddy.

Robert Hoggins

I first saw Ken Dodd on one of the pier shows in Blackpool when I was 14 years old - 60 years ago. He earned himself a new fan that day. What a performer!

Estelle Lewis

Cont.

I saw him live at s theatre show and I laughed so much I couldn't get my breath and had to be treated by St John ambulance on duty at the theatre in the interval. Ken came down to the first aid room to see me, it made my night I'll never forget it!

Andy Bradford

I once offered Doddy a lift home from the local Barber we shared, and he said 'yes, but unless you're a licenced taxi I won't pay you!'. Haha, I said it'll be an honour, when I dropped him off he said "same time in 4 weeks" lol.

Paul Smith Liverpool

A KEN Dodd superfan completed a 100-mile round trip today to say goodbye to his comedy hero.

And Samuel Ball revealed his love for the legendary Liverpool star helped him through tough times of bullying when he was growing up.

Now, 28, the radio presenter keeps an impressive collection of Doddy memorabilia, with around 60 items including records, theatre programmes, Diddy Men dolls and, of course, a tickling stick.

Samuel, up in Merseyside from his home in Stoke, got up at 6am to get ready for the Knotty Ash funnyman's last farewell.

And he laid flowers outside Sir Ken's home before heading for a packed Anglican Cathedral in the city centre .

Samuel said: "I was in high school and I was going through a really, really bad stage of bullying. I had to move schools.

"I remember my mum and dad had an Audience with Ken Dodd on video and I watched it.

"I always loved acting, singing and comedy and, for me going through that stage, he was one of those people who brought a bit of happiness into a dark situation.

"When you go through those things growing up, he's always been a face of hope."

Samuel has been building his collection for three years and said his favourites are the theatre programmes from Doddy's shows over the years.

Cont.

He hopes to eventually pass everything on to the next generation of fans.

He said: "Hopefully, I'll be a parent one day. My wife and I are hoping to have kids.

"He or she will never get to see Sir Ken live but I will be able to show them what he was like.

"I've got records, theatre programmes, badges – and a tickling stick of course – and I've kept an eye on eBay for other things. My wife is very patient!"

Samuel finally met Sir Ken before his show in Warrington in January last year.

He said Doddy, then 89, was amused he and wife Catherine had been waiting outside in the cold for him.

He said: "He signed something to the 'two crazy people'! It was very cold indeed. "He was due on stage in an hour but he had all the time in the world for us. We had a picture taken and joked with him "I wanted to meet him and thank him for giving me so much hope."

Reproduced here with the kind permission of Luke Traynor (The Liverpool Echo)

Fan's Tribute

Today was a gorgeous day in Liverpool, after I left the library earlier this afternoon to go for a coffee, I met 2 wonderful ladies.

They were sitting outside Sayers in London Road having a nice afternoon cuppa in the sun, when I heard one of them say 'Knotty Ash'

Well my ears pricked up when I heard those words, Liverpool being Liverpool, you can approach anyone for a chat! So I said them 'Knotty Ash eh...did you know The Squire then?'

'Yes and we loved him' came the excited reply!!

They informed me they lived in Knotty Ash and bumped into Ken many times and drove past his house every day. They gleefully remembered how Ken would wave to them if he was in his garden and they drove past blowing the car horn! He was always happy to stop and chat whenever they met him.

We spoke about Ken for about half an hour, their admiration for him was so apparent and genuine.

They admired Ken for simply being 'one of us' and despite the fact he could have chosen to live anywhere in the world he stayed loyal to his hometown roots.

After we hugged and I left, it struck me *that* experience was exactly Ken's legacy, he had the gift to bring people together, to make them happy, to connect, a *rare* gift indeed, just as today's chance meeting with 2 fans proved!

I have lived in Liverpool all my life, I have seen many home grown stars come and go and some sadly pass away.

Cont.

In my opinion however, Doddy is the only person that I can start a conversation about with 2 strangers and get that guaranteed response I got today!!

I.e. Everybody in Liverpool loves The Squire and his legacy is safe in Liverpool's hands forever (and everywhere else of course!)

Mike Bartram

Doddy will be greatly missed.I Took my Mum to see him years ago and never laughed so much in my life! He had me in stitches with one of his 1st simplistic jokes... "I went into a Pet Shop and said 'I'd like to buy a fly please' 'sorry sir, we don't sell flies' I said 'well you've got one in the window!' We got out of the theatre after midnight and my sides were sore with laughing.

Magsy Bolan Nolan

When Ken passed away our local radio was speaking to the manager of our local theatre where he was at Xmas, he said that every year he would say to Doddy 'same time next year' and every time Ken would say 'yep same time same place', only this time Ken just looked at him and smiled but didn't say anything, makes you wonder if Ken knew deep down.

Tina Molly

I remember when in the early 80s Ken's car got broken into and Dicky Mint was taken in the theft.

Then some week's later two children playing found dicky mint on waste ground by the Anglican cathedral.

They took Dicky to the police station, he was dirty and his clothes torn and was handed back to Ken. Ken treated those children as a way of thanking them. I remember seeing it in the papers and on the news.

Vera Yorke

Cont.

I was one of his Diddymen from 1984-1994 (age 7-14 ish) and has the sheer joy of being on the Royal Variety Shows, Palladium, panto and This is Your Life and I will never forget after every show we did all year round, and because we had to leave the theatre by 10:30pm, he used to give us (Miss Russell) chip money so that we could get food on the way home. Sometimes there was a few hours' drive home so those chips always went down well!

Such a small gesture that we all loved him for.

Kimberley Reeve (Mills)

I have seen Ken in concert and met Doddy a few times. Always great shows and wonderful to meet Doddy after them. I have a signed photo that Ken Dodd gave to me, and a photo of me and Doddy. I have now got them framed together next to my bed. I will never forget Doddy.

Mr.Alan Penfold.

THE GRAND AND DODDY

The Blackpool Grand stately and fine
Standing on Church street for many a time.

Opened its doors in 1884
Designed by Frank Matchum
A masterpiece for sure.

It cost 20,000 money well spent
Bringing the finest entertainment
To all those that went.

Bought by the Tower in 1909
And business was brisk
This was a great little theatre
Without any risk.

Hard times came knocking in 72
The theatre was in danger from a department store
Or two.

Let's knock down The Grand went out the cry
The land will be useful by and by.

Not likely said some friends of the Grand
They fought the idea by making a stand.

We need a champion to help us raise cash
Someone well known is what we need
So in came 0ur Doddy superb choice indeed
Working so hard tireless and true
He helped put the lights on
Red,White and Blue.

Cont.

The Grand was his home
And that was for sure
Every October he gave us what for.

The king was in residence
And we all lapped it up
Out by midnight
No such luck.

The lights in the theatre
Are now sadly dimmed
In tribute to Doddy
The Jester,The Master
The king.

Now with the angels
Its good luck to them
Will he ever come off at a quarter to ten?

Now we have lost him
He will always be Sir
But when thinking about him at times now and then
Only one name to remember
Simply our KEN.

Michael Harrington

Pam Schuler

Allan Taylor

Christine & Gerry Barnes

Sam Jephcote

Juliana Campbell & Vera Dolan

Productions **itv** Productions

F2

ARKINSON
dnesday 20th June

RS OPEN 5.30pm
RS CLOSE 6.00pm
tly no admittance aft
H 8.00pm approx.

LONDON TELEVISION
R GROUND, LONDON

no admittance to anyone
tography or mobile phon

IT ONE

PARKINSO
on
Wednesday 20th J

Pre-Show
Green Room

DOORS OPEN 5.30pm
DOORS CLOSE 6.00pm
Strictly no admittance after 6.00pm
FINISH 8.00pm approx.
at
THE LONDON TELEVISION CENTRE
UPPER GROUND, LONDON SE1 9LT

Strictly no admittance to anyone under the age of 18
No photography or mobile phones in the studio please

ADMIT ONE

No. 0134

Lynsay Pollard

Sir Ken Dodd embodies all that is great about Great Britain. Nowadays commentators say everything is amazing, fantastic and brilliant and TV personalities are national treasures. However, there is no-one like Ken Dodd for sheer professionalism, longevity and wonderful spiritedness. As funny and kind a man at the stage door as on the stage.

His Happiness Shows were 5 hours of sheer joy and you left aching with laughter but on a wave of joy and love. His audiences adored him because they have grown up and old with him and because his show was an experience good for the soul. I have seen him a dozen times and know some of the jokes but we keep going back each year to Eastbourne because he is unique and we feel so uplifted afterwards.

God Bless Sir Ken.

As Roy Hudd said "the greatest stand-up comedian this country has ever produced". Thank you Ken for the happiness. As one of your younger fans you made us understand what a real star was but with total humility and kindness. We met you in Eastbourne and gave you some Eccles cakes and you always had time for everyone even at 2am in the morning. Now every time I eat one I think of you. I have dreaded this day coming but you will never be forgotten. God Bless you and Lady Anne.

Oliver Pereira

Cont.

Dear Sir Ken,

What a wonderful, kind Gentleman. So genuine, gifted, funny and always such a pleasure to talk to. You are irreplaceable. Thank you for all the happiness and kindnesses - I will remember you always. Until we meet again dearest Absent Friend lots of love and hugs.

Jenny Richardson, Newcastle, Staffordshire

Ken. You were truly one of a kind. The world will be a much sadder place without you but your legacy and the many, many memories and many hours of entertainment you provided all of us, your fans with, will last forever. Thank you for all the laughter and happiness. Much love forever.

Andy Cain, (Sheffield) xxx

A LIGHT'S GONE OUT

Around Knotty Ash I made my way.

Loss of a light then harmed the day.

In its place I think I heard a bell.

God called Doddy, I could kind of tell.

His time had come, a 'journey's end'

Time for fans for a shoulder to lend.

Sure enough, the sad news on TV.

Gone was our Doddy, a hero to me.

Out went a light in Liverpool fourteen.

No more Ken Dodd, a laughter machine!

Everyone loved our Knotty Ash Squire.

Of this unique genius I will never tire.

Under a darkened sky tears were shed.

That light went on in Heaven instead.

Mike Bartram

Not For Me

The sun shone today over Knotty Ash.

No darkened clouds to collide or clash.

The perfect July day some might say.

Yes the sun today had all its own way!

On that 'perfect day' the sun now sets.

Some they say 'that's as good as it gets'

But the tired old sun now says 'tatty Bye'

As the moon peeks into the summer sky.

But it *wasn't* the 'perfect day' not for me.

In Knotty Ash especially it just couldn't be.

Something magical was missing for sure.

No Doddy, just farewell cards by his door.

Mike Bartram

Missing Out

Sunday night, we'd turn on our rented TV.
Put a tanner in the meter and turn the key!
I'd sit with my Mum, infront of the screen.
That was our Sunday night family routine.

Back in those days, a little boy I was then.
About to watch Doddy and his Diddymen.
I felt all grown up, because I stayed up late.
For those Sunday nights, I could hardly wait!

I loved Ken Dodd, from day one I was a fan.
How could you not love such a funny man?
His teeth made me laugh, his sticky up hair.
His tickling sticks that he waved in the air!

The Diddymen came on with funny names.
They sang and danced and played silly games.
I would laugh so much right from the start.
Then Ken would sing, my Mums favourite part!

I think today's young children are missing out.
There are no great comedians to shout about.
A Television in every room, with channels galore.
But nothing can beat those old days for sure!

Mike Bartram

Must have been just after that concert (Victoria Hall, 16/12/17) he caught a bout of flu over Christmas which developed into the chest infection that eventually took his life. He looked quite frail on this video! I never was lucky enough to get to one of his concerts as I've never had the money to afford to, but he came across as a lovely kind sort of man, and he had a lovely singing voice. I always used to enjoy watching Ken on TV, and although I never met him or knew him personally I really feel his loss. We have lost a wonderful entertainer that can never be replaced! RIP dear Ken! Miss You!

Hazel Wykes

He carried on right until the end. He was a wonderful man, his legacy will live on forever

Jade Melissa x

I was also at the Victoria Hall that night with my Mum and Dad. We were sitting on the front row in the first circle down the left side near to the stage.

Rachel Emily Parkes

My little story is about Knotty Ash. In the 90s my partner and I were driving up to Manchester, and somehow missed the junction and ended up in Liverpool, and driving through Knotty Ash. I joked that we should call on Ken for a cuppa and a jam butty! He was quite stressed so didn't see the funny side at the time, but we often laugh about it now!

Stephanie Baker

Cont.

No one comes close to Doddy, he was a one off. I have never heard of anyone as wonderful to fans off stage as Sir Ken. Making people happy was what he lived for. God bless him.

Scarlett Flowers x

Sir Doddy *MUST BE* on stage in heaven, making the Angels and St.Peter cry with laughter.... It has been raining here in Runcorn since about 9pm last night!

Amanda.L. Lewis-Jones

It is such a pity that Ken was not knighted long ago. His knighthood was far too long in coming, and I think no-one deserved the title more than him. I am glad that his lovely wife is now his "Lady" in every sense of the word.

Elaine Baddeley

Fans' Tributes

Ken Dodd holds box office records for theatres all over the country, and many of these date back to the 1960s. He still holds the record for summer season at the Opera House in Blackpool, and always will for it isn't record receipts at the box office its bums on seats. Summer season used to start at the spring bank holiday in May and go through to the end of the lights at the start of November. There were two shows a night, six nights of the week.

I think the Opera House seats 3,300, not sure exactly, but I remember a plaque on the wall that said it was licensed to accommodate 87 people standing at the back of the stalls and 56 standing at the back of the circle. Every night there were people standing at the second house of Ken's show. Not until all of these people were in did the "house full" notice go up outside and it was there to be seen every night.

I daresay Health and Safety may have done away with the standing permit even in spite of the place having very wide aisles. You'd to be off your mark if you wanted any of the 36,000+ tickets a week. Arrive at your hotel, put the luggage in and head down to the Winter Gardens to see which box office had the shortest queue! Just look at the number of members of the Appreciation Society who have been fans since 'way back then, like myself. I cannot think of any other entertainer who inspired such love and loyalty from his audiences.

Sandra Wallace

I was driving home from a Ken show very early in the morning i.e. 3.30 am and got lost a police car came by and stopped to ask if I was ok. I said I was lost and he asked what I was doing out alone at this time of night. I said I was trying to get home after being at a Ken Dodd show.

His reply was 'Oh hell does he do bed and breakfast now?'

I told Ken the story and he laughed his head off and said you must be the only person to get a police escort home from my show!

But they did only take me to the M6!

Rosemarie Jones

I remember one joke he told me when there was just both of us in the Barbers... he said "did you see the local news last night? I said 'no Ken'...he said "terrible news the lollipop man from the school down the road was sacked" I didn't even know it was a joke and said 'no I didn't, what for'? ....'for working on the side' came the reply (you might have to be from Liverpool to understand it I think)

Paul Smith Liverpool

I used to work in a care home as an activities coordinator, one afternoon. I put a Ken Dodd DVD on the TV and handed round some tickling sticks, and just sat and watched 20 people's faces turn into Happy faces, they enjoyed every minute of it xxx

Denise Best

Cont.

I heard Doddy caused a riot while they were recording Mastermind. I heard after each person had their turn in the black chair, Ken stood up and started telling jokes to the audience, they had to keep re taking it I believe, whether this is true or not I don't know!

Irene Walsh

Ken was a master of comedy and he will be sorely missed by millions. May you rest in peace Ken.

Dave Bourne

Ken Dodd wasn't just a comedian, or a rapid-fire *Joke-Machine*; rather he was a Zany Jester of Wizard dimensions, who combined his never-ending comedic-extravaganzas with the emotive and the heart-rending pathos of Grimaldi!

Gerry George

FOR THE SQUIRE

For decades our Doody owned the crown.

Only one King, be it comic, singer or clown.

Respected and so admired by his fellow pro.

The 'comedian's comedian' his record will show.

He rose the entertainment and comedy bar.

Ever so gracious and humble, although a star.

Shows that he performed well into the night.

Quick fire style, much to his audience delight!

Understood exactly what made his audience tick.

Innovative, he perfected every comedy trick!

Rest in peace Ken Dodd, your nation has cried.

Every 'absent friend' will now be by your side.

Mike Bartram

Scouse Pride

I love The Beatles, the amazing 'Fab Four!
My scouse heroes, I have got them galore.
From the world of entertainment and of sport.
So much joy, my scouse heroes have brought!

Number one Liverpool records, what a haul.
Just Look at that plaque on the Cavern Wall!
Cilla, Gerry Marsden, Frankie to name a few.
And the singing sensation, our Ken Dodd too!

Liverpool artists have produced big hit after hit.
As for comedy, we are renowned for our wit!
But egos can take over in the world of fame.
So meeting your heroes is a dangerous game.

But although he wore the King of comedy crown.
One such artist would never let his fans down.
A humble, caring man, kindness personified.
That's why Doddy fills me *most* with scouse pride!

Mike Bartram

A Tribute to Sir Ken Dodd.

I was first aware of Sir Ken when he came to The Granada Theatre Shrewsbury in October 1956 and have loved him ever since. He used to come to our Hospital Social club at the Royal Shrewsbury Hospital where he invited me on stage to do some daft things with his tickling sticks it was wonderful.

Since then I have seen his shows in various parts of the country never missing a show in Shrewsbury the last time in June 2017 when I was again mentioned by Ken I had asked him if he would sing Absent Friends. I was delighted when he did but afraid I cried all the way through I had a feeling this would be the last time I would see him.

A few years ago I made him a walking stick I do hope it was some help during his illness Sir Ken Dodd a wonderful comedian you could take your Grandmother and Grandchildren to see him knowing there would be no bad language or offensive material to upset. What a man he will be missed so much and especially that wonderful voice. Sir Ken you were loved by everyone

Rest In Peace.   Phyllis Edwards   (Stickmaker) Shrewsbury, Shropshire.

A man who set an example to us all of how to make our way through life and find joy and happiness in the simple things. Genuinely kind, considerate and a decent human being. He thoroughly deserved the adoration of his fans. So glad he knew how much he was loved.

Jan Rawlings

Cont.

Before class today in Toronto, Canada, I told my students, who come together from all over the world, that my favourite Liverpool comedian, entertainer & legend had passed away. They were insistent on seeing a video of him so we watched an online clip of Ken singing Quando Caliente — to say the room was filled with the sound of laughter would be an understatement. Thank you again Ken for a lifetime of laughs, goodnight and God bless to you, your Lady and family.

Steven, Toronto, Canada

Happy Memories of when I worked on the Ken Dodd show at The Crewe Lyceum Theatre, Ken was a top bloke who always had time for everyone including the stage crew and fellow spot ops.

Johnathan Hulse.

One evening at the Theatre Royal in Saint Helens there were only four backstage staff working a Doddy night shift near Christmas. I say 'night shif't as the 7.30pm audience left at 11.30pm and the 10pm audience got in 11.45pm and left at 2am!

Backstage the stage manager had old photos of stars and one was Doddy with a cigarette in his hand. Doddy wanted to buy the photograph because he'd stop smoking and wanted no reminders. The stage manager refused to sell but did take it down off display. With only the Stage Manager and myself there Anne gave us both a Christmas tip of £10.00 each. The largest tip I think we ever got!

Chatting backstage after audience departed Ken said to me "Son. Those bad jokes you tell deserve someone who can deliver them better. Your delivery is all wrong. Try my friend Jimmy Tarbuck"

That to me was a great thing when a legend doesn't ridicule your humour but tries to improve it. Ken was not only a gentleman but mentor to many.

Derek Ashworth

Cont.

I met him. I thought he was wonderful before I met him but after…well, I was so full of admiration and respect I thought I would burst! He was all like you have read about him, and more. Witty, considerate, gifted, self-effacing, respectful unique and so on. I loved him when I was 12 and my illusion was only enforced by working with him 40 years later. Wonderful man.

Glynis Kester-Page

I remember Sir Ken walking my husband Jim and I to the train station after lunch on our annual visit to the UK from California. I bought Ken a small frying pan. Ken, "Missus, By Jove it's just what I wanted a Diddy frying pan" as he laughed. I'm laughing now, what was I thinking?

Pamela Schuler

A wonderful occasion when my friend Rosemarie Jones and I travelled to London to see Ken at the Royal variety show at the Coliseum. It was a fabulous night and we saw Charles and Camilla close up as they arrived. After we saw all the stars leaving and Meatloaf spent more time than most with the fans. Ken was lovely and I got some great shots of him as he and Anne were leaving for the after show party.

Lynsay Pollard

Here's my short account of when I met our hero. I had bumped into him a few times in Sainsbury's in Knotty Ash, just to say a quick hello, 'Hello young man' he would always say back, and asked how I was etc. He was always impeccably dressed and so polite.

For those who know the Liverpool area, I met Doddy again in Tesco on Queens Drive, this time it was for a 10 minute chat! Hello young man he said (love the young man bit, I am 60 this year) he was as elegant and charming as ever. 'You're a big fella' he said' 'l would hate to keep you in chips'!

He laughed at my shorts and legs (haha, with good reason I suppose!) I asked him if he would kindly say hello to my Mum, Doddy agreed of course without hesitation. I said it would be over the phone though, he didn't mind waiting while I called my Mum on my mobile. He spoke to my Mum and asked her if she knew how her son was dressed while he was out in public. He was as witty as ever!!

Finally, I told Doddy I was on the way to Leeds and just getting petrol, 'Goodbye and safe journey young man' he said...absolutely buzzing all the way to Leeds. 'Never meet your heroes' they say, maybe so...but not when your hero is Doddy!!

Mike Bartram

Saw doddy about 4 "times... Had to leave early once cos I had to be up for work as a postie!

Terry Hughes

Cont.

I'm a postie too, but on collections. When I told Ken what I did he told me to be careful when out driving. Awww. He was so lovely.

Helen McIntyre

I met Ken Dodd while working for the BBC a few years ago. I was lucky enough to go backstage during the interval at one of his gigs in Birmingham. He was lovely and friendly from the start. He decided there and then that he would call me Gypsy Rose lol.

He didn't mind when I watched him putting on his make-up while telling me that the tin box containing his stage make-up had been with him from the start of his career. It was old and battered but he said he would never part with it. He gave me a signed tickling stick for my partner Marc and a signed photo. He kissed me goodbye. He was the loveliest of men and very funny. I came away feeling like he had always been a good friend.

Karen Bond

On holiday in Blackpool in the 60s, when the theatres did two performances a night. At changeover time Church Street was packed, with 4 theatres within about 150 yards. One evening our parents told us to stand in a shop doorway out of the way of the crowd. We were across from the Opera House where Ken was starring. I looked up and there was a man on the roof, on a sort of inspection platform.

He was drinking a cup of tea and looking up and down the street at all the people. Dad said it was Ken. We saw him several times, often there was a lady with him- Anita. Fast forward many years and I was speaking to Ken after a show in Edinburgh. Blackpool was mentioned and Ken said Blackpool and the Opera House were very special favourites because of all the great times he'd had there. Then he said he used to love to watch all the people out to go to the theatres and to think that he'd played a part in giving them pleasure.

His favourite view in Blackpool was from the top of the Opera House. I asked if he stood out on a platform, and I'll never forget the joy in his eyes and the 1000 watt smile at that memory and to think he'd been spotted! His little dog, Doodle, had come out with him to meet us that night and on the mention of Blackpool Doodle sat down. Ken said he had learned that 'Blackpool' meant he'd be here for a wee while yet!

Sandra Wallace

To Ken

Gone are the days of how tickled you are.

Gone are the Diddy men.

Gone is your smile.

Gone are the tickling sticks.

No matter what, you're never gone in

our hearts.

You gave us "Happiness" now all that's

left are our "Tears"

Thank you Sir Ken for all you have done.

Even though you're the most loved of all "Absent Friends"

The Heavens are glowing with glory.

Hark! The laughter of angels and a choir

rejoice in harmony.

Long may you reign as King of Comedy.

Shanai Eliza Jane Collins

A Concert Ticket (If Only So)

I look at this concert ticket, and think 'if only so.'

But that night there would be no Ken Dodd show.

Well there *will* be a show, just at a venue new.

Where all his absent friends will get the best view!

I think of Doddy and all the Theatres he played.

To play them all, was a wish Doddy once made.

Those Theatres now lack some sparkle and glow.

How I wish so much our Doddy didn't have to go.

I look at this concert ticket, its stub still intact.

Another sell out show, yet another theatre packed.

Laughter galore, from once the lights dimmed low.

I look at this concert ticket, and think 'if only so.'

Mike Bartram

God's Plan

Now a month since Doddy passed away.

I still think of the Squire most every day.

The jokes, the songs, a package complete.

The laughter rising from every filled seat.

Now with social media to keep in touch.

Fans can mix, and be friends and such.

Heartfelt stories which fans can share.

Funny encounters about Doddy, our sir.

And no scandal in the gutter press to read.

No sensationalist stories sold for greed.

No shocking headlines to help papers sell.

As simply there are no such stories to tell.

Because Ken Dodd wasn't that kind of man.

Just a lovely bloke who stuck to Gods' plan.

The plan why Ken was put on Gods' earth?

Was to share happiness for all he was worth!

Mike Bartram

I would love to share a very personal moment with you all if that's ok? I was 18 years old when my mum died after being very ill for much of my childhood, as you can imagine I was in a fog and thought the world had ended and that I would never smile again. I ended up walking round the estate where we lived on that horrible day and several folk wanted me to come into their houses obviously they heard about mum dying.

I wandered around until I went to my auntie's house the family there were having their evening meal and were all in the kitchen. Auntie made me a brew of tea and gave me a sandwich and then went to turn the television off but I said no because at that time Ken was on doing what he did best. Ken made me laugh on the very day I thought I would never laugh again.

I wrote to him and told him this and received a lovely letter back with an invitation to go back stage and meet him. I never got to see him. I am 63 years old now and I will never forget this Angel we know as Sir Ken Dodd God bless thank you for reading this xx There will NEVER be anyone like him again GENIUS xx

Ruth Callaghan

I live in New Zealand & under the umbrella of The Billy Fury Fan Club I have raised thousands of dollars for charity for many years - shows - a bit like Stars in their eyes but with a different theme each show. One 3 hr show 'Around The World on BILLYair' we went around the world & OF COURSE we HAD to make a stop in Liverpool. I searched for ages to find a copy of Doddy's Little Diddy Men (pre YouTube) - with no

Cont.

luck. Eventually (having no address for Ken) I sent a letter addressed to: Ken Dodd, Knotty Ash, Liverpool - telling him about my plight. Back came a tape of Doddy's Little Diddy Men & a beautiful letter from Ken himself typed on an old typewriter. I will never forget his kindness. Bless This Scouse! I did send him a video of the show. Ironic that both Ken & My Billy both have statues in Liverpool.

Moya Gleave

New Zealand

One Wish

If I was given one wish, just one desire.

I'd wish one more show from the Squire.

That seems very selfish, but there you go.

Just love to see one more Doddy show!

If just the one wish was granted to me.

Yes I *should* wish for world harmony.

But how long would that harmony last?

Always one more missile primed to blast.

So one more Ken show my wish for sure.

A million in the audience, no safely law!

You might say, wishes never come true!

But tonight in my dreams, I hope mine do!

Mike Bartram

Hand in Hand

Irrelevant or insignificant the old days classed.

Dismissed far too often does become our past.

Buildings, places, stars of music, screen or stage.

You see them sadly resigned to a forgotten page.

It happens more and more, much to my dismay.

The past ignored, a distant memory, hazy or grey.

But our Doddy will never become a victim of this.

As such a legend would be impossible to dismiss.

Fashions, with time I've seen them come and go.

Trends, appear and vanish just like melting snow.

But the test of time our Doddys' legacy will stand.

As the future and Ken Dodd will go hand in hand.

Mike Bartram

Ken Dodd Poem

Thank you God for giving us Ken.
And his smiling diddymen.
Loved by young and old the same.
And unaffected by his fame.
Thank you God for giving us Ken
Who brought us so much 'Happiness'
He made us laugh until we cried.
And 'Tears' when we heard that he'd died.
Thank you God for giving us Ken.
Who was everybody's friend.
A kind and thoughtful family man.
Assisted by his lovely 'Anne'
Thank you God for giving us Ken.
Proudest Liverpudlian.
An honest scouser through and through.
To his great city always true.
Thank you God for giving us Ken.
The likes of which we'll never see again.
A loss for us still left on earth.
Who always gave us our money's worth.
Thank you God for giving us Ken.
Now making people laugh in Heaven.
How tickled he will always be.
Glorious, 'tattyfilariously'!
Thank you God for giving us Ken.
Who made us all feel like children.
He made us lose all track of time.
A star that will for ever shine.

Peter Lewis

Thank you for the laughter and memorable songs Ken. I watched you with my granny and granddad through the 50's and 60's; with my daughter in the 80's and 90's, and now with my grandsons.

We'll always hold you dearly in our hearts.

Love from Linda Binns and family, Trawden, Lancashire.

Chin up Anne. Xxx

I saw you three times and it was a laugh a minute.
Thank you for making this world a happier place.
The best comedian and human being ever.

Thanks, Chris Malone (Bolton)

I can hear the angels laughing all the way over in Lincolnshire. Many thanks to Ken for so many years of laughter. I should say R.I.P. but I can't see you doing that so keep those angels laughing.

Dave and Sue Delve.

Scousers in Spalding

Ken was truly a one-of-a-kind. There will be no more like him.

I travelled from Los Angeles to New Brighton, twice in the past few years to see his show.

Cont.

157

Totally worth the travel to see a comedy genius at work for 5 hours each time!

Rest in peace, Sir Ken.

**David Gregory
LA, USA**

Thank you Ken for all the ... Happiness ... you have given over the years.

Love. Pauline Fitton.

Tweed Heads Australia

Columbus was a famous man;

Einstein was one, too.

They were known to all, but then,

Along came you.

Davy Crockett, he could hunt;

Betsy Ross could sew,

But your fine qualities outshine them all;

You're the greatest one we know.

Love and miss you every day.

Irene Walsh

Tribute to Sir Ken Dodd

Our absent Friend

The love of his fans.

The Squire of Knotty Ash

The King of Comedy.

The Sir Knight of Liverpool

The Diddy of the Diddymen.

The tenor voice of Sir Ken

The laughter of our Doddy.

Sir Kenneth Arthur Dodd has his

Lady Anne Dodd to continue

Sharing her husband memories

With his fans and friends.

AMEN

Pam Schuler

Doddy Poem

I've always been a Doddy fan,
I watched him on TV
I listened to his lovely songs
Since I was two or three.
But to his show I'd never been
so for a little treat,
I bought myself a ticket,
and sat happily in my seat.
The band struck up, the lights came on
The audience cheered out loud
as Ken appeared upon the stage
and made friends with the crowd.
He told his jokes, he sang his songs,
By Jove we had a ball
The minutes turned to hours
before his final curtain call!
Now he's so sadly left us
as to heaven he departs,
But we'll never forget our Doddy
as he'll live on in our hearts.

Susie Watts

TILL DAWN

Tomorrow another day since our loss.

Incredible tributes I have come across.

Loving and sincere, from many a heart.

Loved our Doddy, a class miles apart.

Dawn of course tomorrow will still come.

Always a new day, always a new Sun.

When today's Sun decides to set.

No tears of ours will have dried just yet.

Mike Bartram

Southport Theatre

12/5/18

On Saturday I'll be on Southport Pier.

And during my visit I will leave a tear.

The Southport Theatre, its stage bare.

No Happiness show for fans to share.

No Doddy, no Dicky, no laughs galore.

No beautiful songs we'd hear for sure.

No overtime that night for Theatre staff!

For the full house, no midnight laugh.

But on Saturday that visit I'll *still* make.

In memory of Doddy, flowers I'll take.

Mike Bartram

Fans' Tributes

I met Ken in the 50's, Alhambra Theatre, UK.

I fell in love with his music "Pianissimo, Love Is Like A Violin, Once In Every Lifetime." Molly my friend went backstage, met Ken, he mentioned he would be in Manchester. We called the theatre told them Ken told us to call. We had front seats guests of Ken Dodd and went back stage. After the show, Ken was excited to see us, handed someone money to go out and buy Champagne for my friends. We toasted I couldn't stop laughing. The conductor on the train told us to behave ourselves when we couldn't stop laughing, we told him this was our first alcoholic drink with Ken Dodd. Then the conductor started laughing too!

Pam Schuler

Ken never needed to use foul language to get his point across! He could make you laugh just by his expression alone!

Nanna Fran Howe

That was the genius of the man that he didn't need to use foul language to make us not just laugh but have our sides aching, absolutely superb and he had no peer in my humble opinion.

Stewart Sherwin

I last met him after his show last November in Hull where he gave me (and my mum) a tickling stick. They are very treasured possessions

Cont.

Along with the obvious of being a fantastic entertainer, Ken was such a lovely, kind, caring and thoughtful gentleman who was genuinely interested in his fans. He was always concerned with if we were ok getting home and last year, he and Anne drove slowly in the car, waving as they went past, making sure we got to my car safely.

Helen McIntyre

The Knotty Ash Primary School Fete took place each year organised by St. John's church and Ken always came and supported us. He would spend hours talking to all those who came. His love and encouragement for people was second to none. And as his vicar he would chat openly with me about the community he loved and the importance of faith.

Roy Doran

Many years ago, when we came to live in North Wales, we were investigated by the Inland Revenue. Eventually 2 people from the Tax office came to our house, our accountant was there also, and as they came in the front door we had Ken on singing "Tears". Our accountant said it was a bad idea, we said it was our house and we'd play what we wanted. No further issues with the revenue and I told Ken this tale when I met him years later backstage at Venue Cymru. With his brush with that lot he was quite amused to say the least. He was brilliant and will live on forever.

Grace Kelly

It's Jam Butty o'Clock!

Dicky Mint is the Head Timekeeper
of the Diddymen of Knotty Ash,
who work in the Jam Butty Mines,
the Treacle Wells,
the Broken Biscuit Repair Works
and the Black Pudding Plantation.

A very industrious town indeed.

Courtesy of Rosemarie Jones

Fan's Tribute

Many have wondered what kept Ken Dodd going. Where did he get the energy and stamina to do those wonderful Marathon shows?

Well, I'm going try and explain to you wonderful people...

I have been an entertainer, Comedian and Magician for over 25 years. Thanks to the Man himself, Our Doddy.

I have the same work ethos as him. Entertaining people is our lifeblood!

So what does that mean? Well, very often you are going to do a show and you are not feeling well, sometimes very ill! Or in a lot of pain!

Earlier in the day you REALLY don't feel like doing that show. But you never let an audience down!

As the preparation for it starts, especially in a theatre.... You hear the call bells... Half an Hour... 10 Minutes...5 Minutes., Your blood starts pumping.

By the time the last call bell rings and your entrance music is playing..... YOU HAVE NO PAIN! TRUE...!! NONE.

YOU DON'T FEEL ILL! NOPE Not a bit...

And if you can get that audience in the palm of your hand, you feel invincible, you could do anything. You feel 18 again!

You then see the change in your audience, the pleasant affect you have on them. They change from sullen, sometimes sad to animated, alive, happy, rejuvenated!

Then you feel the energy, the connection, the love. It's wonderful! It's Better than sex!!............. Unless I've been doing that bit wrong.

Cont.

THEN... you finish. ....

The people give their thanks by way of applause, some come for autographs and photos.

IF you are lucky the show high can last a few hours more. Then you head home.

Looking forward to the next show where you feel Loved and ALIVE!

THAT my friends is, was Ken Dodd.

I have been backstage during a show and you could see that distinct change in him!

He bumbles into the wings WITH either A pint or cup of tea in hand... a bit slumped...just like a guy relaxing in his own kitchen.

Then the last call bell rings and the Doddy Orchestra stops their interlude. There's a crash of symbols!

His face changes...it's like he inflates and becomes Sharper. Taller. He straightens and a light, that twinkle comes into his eyes!

Anne gives him a kiss and starts her introduction......... "Star of the Palladium. King of the Diddymen,............... Kennnnn Dodd!"

BOOM!! This shuffling ordinary looking man becomes a light footed ball of energy! Striding on stage with the energy of someone half his age.

Entertainment was his lifeblood! Better than ANY painkiller or drug! It's what kept him going. It's what kept him young!

He lived for the love of his Audience and the audience Loved him for it!

Our Doddy, Forever Young. God Bless you x

Donna Collins (Gladys ChuckleButty)

On one occasion before a show in Nottingham, Ken came out to talk to people. It was a warm summer evening and Ken called me over. He was recording Another Audience with Ken Dodd and asked if I would be in the audience as he wanted real fans there. I took my daughter Sarah and a friend of Ken's Geoff Quible. It was a memorable evening I will never forget. I went to this with my husband and afterwards were invited to the green room where we chatted with Parky (Michael Parkinson), Ken and Anne and Ken's script writer John Pye and his wife. Sadly John later died. A wonderful night that will live with me forever.

Lynsay Pollard

Ken not only appreciated other comedians, he appreciated everyone he met, a rare gift indeed!

Peter Lew

In the few fleeting meetings I had with him - the most surprising thing to me being, that he was such a charming, well-focused and confidently-articulate gentleman!

Gerry George

Who can EVER come REMOTELY CLOSE to THE Squire of Knotty Ash?

Amanda.L. Lewis-Jones

Cont.

No one...As well as a fabulous all round entertainer, Ken was such a kind, thoughtful caring man who always had time for his fans.

Helen McIntyre

No one.... Not a soul comes close x

Iris Williams

When my husband was in hospital in 1989 I called Sir Ken. Sir Ken gave me comfort which helped me and Jim got well. March 24, 1995 I asked Sir Ken if he would send my mother a birthday card for 80th she was admitted into a nursing home. Sir Ken autographed and sent my mother a card which my mother was so happy she said she felt like a Queen. October 29th 1995 Sunday 11:30a.m. My mother passed away. I called Sir Ken gave him my brother & wife address.

A flower bouquet arrangement from Sir Ken was delivered the following day. The little kind things which Sir Ken did are those memories which are close to my heart. I took photos of all the arrangements and brought all my mother's 80th cards including Sir Ken back to the USA. I have kept all my Christmas cards from Sir Ken & Anne for over 40 years. 2018 is going to be hard this year. I will continue sending Lady Anne Dodd Christmas cards now including remembering our friend Sir Ken Dodd.

Pam Schuler

I remember when I was a boy, my shadow small.

With Diddymen wallpaper on my bedroom wall.

Too young to see Doddy and pennies where few.

The internet was merely a dream, TV channels 2!

So Sunday night was special, The Palladium Show.

Doddy would make me laugh, till tears would flow!

'Knotty Ash' became a place that I longed to find.

Where Diddymen roamed, and jam butties where mined.

I would then go to bed happy and I would dream.

Those mines I found, to Knotty Ash I had been!

Doddy became special while my shadow grew tall.

Alas today now my tears for a different reason fall.

Mike Bartram

Well Doddy – what can I say that many famous and far more important people than myself have not already said? My late Grandmother, Mother and Father loved you and so myself and my Brother were brought up in a household that never missed an opportunity to see you perform on the television.....and we loved you! Fast forward some 46 years, and to when I turned 56 I said to my husband "do you know, I want to go and see a live Ken Dodd performance" I just knew I had to do it and experience for myself the comedy genius that was Ken Dodd – and I am so glad that I did. What a privilege to see you at the Embassy Theatre in Skegness back in 2016. My sides were splitting throughout the performance.

What struck me the most though was your sincerity for your audience, and I left the theatre with the most overwhelming feeling of gratitude that I had taken the opportunity to see a Master of his trade thrilling his audience to the point where none of us wanted your show to finish. I want to say 'thank you' a million times for making our lives a brighter place, and indeed in a dark world it takes someone special to help people forget for a little while what uncertain times we live in. I hope you find peace in Paradise – you have more than earned your rest, so for now I will say "tatty bye Doddy" – and thank you for all the laughs and pleasure you gave to so many.

Finally to Lady Anne I would just like to send my deepest sympathy and pray that God will sustain you with so many happy memories of your wonderful husband at this sad time – sincerely, thank you for sharing him with us.

Heather Shipton. Kettering, Northants.

Vacancy

A vacancy has arisen, a new position to fill.
The comedy world needs a new top of the bill.
Audiences need their chuckle muscle strained.
But can anyone replace he who once reigned?

We now have a vacancy, to fill Doddy's shoes.
Anyone spring to mind who you might choose?
A mammoth ask, almost impossible you'd say.
But we do have a vacancy, please apply today.

In saying that, not many comedians need apply.
As you don't measure up, numerous reasons why.
You see it's a unique position we must get it right.
You'll need the qualities of a gentleman knight.

The role involves extra long hours, so be aware.
To the greatest ever comic you'll have to compare.
A mighty challenge indeed, it's an order so tall.
A vacancy has arisen but are you up for the call?

Can you keep your fans for hours spell bound?
As comics go, have you the best voice around?
Do you have staying power, decade on decade?
Can you still shine, while all around you fade?

Now suddenly like magic I've travelled far in time.
I'm in the long distant future in this dream of mine.
And I notice in history that vacancy they didn't fill.
Because Sir Ken Dodd was the King of Comedy still!

Mike Bartram

I have known Ken all my life. He and my father both started out 'in the business' about the same time so I guess that's how they first met. Ken went on to be a great star, my father became a teacher!! Such is life!

I have lots of lovely memories of Ken from when I was a child, he came to our house occasionally, and I remember the wonder and excitement of going to see my famous 'uncle' Ken on stage and later after the show. He always used to call me 'twinkle toes'!!

My father was also a keen potter, and one his hobbies was to make models of the stars of the day. Ken was his first subject, and when he presented him with a model, Kens then fiancée, Anita exclaimed 'ooh look, a diddy Doddy!' Ken later suggested that was part of the inspiration for the diddy men!

As I got older, I began to appreciate the privilege of seeing both sides of Ken, the wonderfully zany comedian on stage, and the intelligent philosopher backstage. He could hold a conversation on any subject, and he and my dad would spend ages 'putting the world to rights'.

When my father passed away, Ken sent a beautiful floral tribute, and a card saying my father had been a good friend and a true gentleman - a lovely tribute.

Since then I continued to follow Ken's career and see him whenever possible- even though I moved to Spain, I still returned to my home town of Southport to go to his show and see him afterwards.

The last time I saw him was at the dinner in London, although we spoke on the phone just before Christmas.

Elaine R Jones

There will never be an entertainer as superb as Sir Ken. When you walked into the theatre and Sir Ken came on the stage, just the sight of him made you feel so very happy. The love he had for people was so evident to see. You were completely captivated by his comedy and songs - which were so poignant - and your face ached with being in hysterics with his jokes.

He possessed the ability to make you forget all your problems and nothing was quite as magical as going to see Sir Ken. The enigma, also, of what time the show would finish was always present!!

I can remember being quite self conscious about going to see Sir Ken as I now have to instil eye drops very frequently, due to chronic dry eyes. Although he saw me doing this, he made no reference to it at all. What a kind, caring and thoughtful man he was.

I am so pleased Sir Ken got his wish that he never retired. Sadly though on the 11 March 2018 we lost such an invaluable entertainer. A huge void has been left in our lives. Thank goodness we will always have the memories to look back on, the books, the CDs and DVDs.

Sir Ken was the most educated, tender and loving person there has ever been in show business. He will always remain a pure legend.

Elaine Robinson

Cont.

I live in California, USA with my husband Jim of 50 years.

I saw the funeral live during the night, 8 hrs behind UK time.

It was like being there through the service, singing the hymns, enjoying the selection of the music.

That was the day I went through my 45's, recorded a song with my cell phone. My Facebook Sunday Memories of Sir Ken began every Sunday. The B side of 'Happiness '...Wow 'I'll Never Forget You'

It's like Sir Ken is singing to each person, I'll never forget him to family, friends, and fans.

Pam Schuler

The World's Best

Famous Liverpool comedians grow on trees!
Arthur Askey, Tommy Handley if you please!
Mick Miller, Tarby and Tom O' Connor as well.
Comics with fantastic jokes and stories to tell.

But one Liverpool born comedian tops the lot.
He's got *that* something that only he has got.
I am talking about our own Doddy of course!
A one man laughter show…a whirlwind force.

An audience in his palm, from curtain rise to fall.
Laughter roaring down from top circle to stall.
Liverpool for comics is worldwide renowned.
But another like Ken Dodd will *never* be found!

And if people ever ask for my reasons why.
My answers will never be in short supply.
Not convinced, just watch vintage Ken on TV.
I'm sure you'll then end up agreeing with me!

Excitement levels soared when Doddy hit Town.
Wherever he played, he wore the comedy crown.
A timeless artist, the best through and through.
Liverpool's best, the Nation's best, the Worlds'
best too!

Mike Bartram

When I was a child growing up I sat glued to the BBC TV every time Dicky Mint, Diddy Evan, Nigel Ponsonby Smallpiece, Harry Cott, Wee Hamish, Mick The Marmaliser and Smarty Arty were on with that 'Funny Man' Ken Dodd. I liked to call him "uncle Doddy"

I always dropped everything to watch him.   Which sometimes meant the rest of the family missed something else on ITV as we only had one television , with a 50p meter on the side from Radio Rentals in our living room, they had no choice!

When I left my childhood home, as I am sure everyone does, they always mean to somehow contact beloved extended family members but never do. That was me with Sir Doddy. I always planned to write him a letter 'TOMORROW' 'NEXT WEEK' 'SOMETIME SOON' when I had time to. I always planned to do so but, in my wanting to respect his privacy, I never did. You see I forgot my Uncle Sir Doddys advice...

'DO NOT PUT OFF UNTIL TOMORROW WHAT YOU CAN DO TODAY. DO IT TODAY AND (IF YOU LIKE IT) YOU CAN DO IT AGAIN TOMORROW.'

Amanda. L. Lewis-Jones.

Magical Knotty Ash

I'd pass Doddys' home most day and night.

And all in the world to me seemed all right.

It just made me happy to pass his home.

Lovely Knotty Ash, with its jam butty zone!

I would be off to work, another night shift.

My flagging spirits sometimes in need of a lift.

I would get that lift knowing Ken was there.

Something magical in the Knotty Ash air!

I would walk my dog, my beautiful Kim.

I'd pass Doddys' house and hope he was in!

Hope I'd see Doddy, even a glimpse to catch!

My comedy hero, nobody will ever match!

When I passed Sir Kens house, all seemed well.

Sir Ken Dodd and Knotty Ash, the perfect gel.

Now I pass his house everyday on Thomas Lane.

And all in my life doesn't feel quite the same.

Mike Bartram

As Chairman of The British Music Hall Society I had the privilege to meet, socialise and work with the great man Sir Ken Dodd many times.

Only on 26th October last year I have the honour of presenting Sir Ken with the British Music Hall Society Lifetime Achievement Award.

Not only was this a great occasion but the night before I dined with Ken & Anne and Roy and Debbie Hudd, how fantastic to share time and a table with such greats.

In 2013 at our 50th Anniversary celebrations at Wilton's Music Hall Roy Hudd interviewed Sir Ken and for a few hour before the interview I shared a dressing room with Sir Ken.

10 minutes before he was due on stage the stage manager came to collect him and escort him to the stage. Ken stood up and Anne said that his tie was very creased, now hanging over a rail were 4 or 5 other ties but Anne turned the iron on....I waited for Ken to take the tie off but he didn't...he simply approached the ironing board, bent down and Anne ironed the tie while he was still wearing it, taking the hot iron within millimetres from his face. I have a photograph of this somewhere.

Adam Borzone

Chairman

British Music Hall Society

Cont.

I was a late comer to Sir Ken. I found his music at a time when I needed something. I lost my Dad in tragic circumstances in 2013 and I went to bed for 3 months. I found his music tremendously uplifting and so I wrote to him. He wrote back. It truly made such a difference to me. I understand from what I've seen and heard since that this was his way. What an extraordinary gentleman in the truest sense of the word.

Georgie Stewart

Sir Ken Dodd is, and will always be my hero. Whilst I was in school, I had to move schools due to bullying. It was around this time I came across Sir Ken's first audience with – I was hooked and his humour, singing and stage presence inspired me to get through that period and pursue a passion for performing.

To this day, I have over 200 pieces of Doddy memorabilia, which gives me great pleasure. There isn't a day that goes by that I don't listen to his music, or watch a performance or show of his online. I felt like a lost a dear friend when he passed, I just thank God for the laughter and light he brought into my life.

Thank you Sir Ken, you'll always inspire me to be myself – and to never take myself too seriously.

Samuel Ball

Curtain Call

I've watched this book grow slowly, page by page.

Dedicated to our Doddy, the comic hero of our age.

I thank you all, who have taken the effort and time.

To contribute your dedications, be it story or rhyme.

And for the many photos, and amazing artwork too!

I've seen some great talent from fans old and new.

To his loyal legion of fans, Doddy always gave his all.

Be it a TV slot or theatre appearance, every curtain call.

This book is our little tribute; from our hearts we say.

Thank you to a comic genius, so unique in every way.

Happiness *and* kindness, Ken Dodd had the gift to share.

The most talented entertainer *ever* and its greatest 'sir'.

Mike Bartram

Fan's Tribute

I have been lucky enough to have followed the genius, Sir Ken Dodd for over a decade. A true gentleman through and through; from his arriving at the theatre, to staying behind after his performance and greeting his followers; ever so jolly and welcoming. He treated everyone as a friend he'd known for years.

With every performance he gave it his all, from his classic one liners, to his duo with Dicky Mint.

There was no other comedian who could have a whole theatre belly laughing from 7pm-1am! His routine will be remembered by all his fans, which is just what he would have wanted.

There will be no other Sir Ken Dodd, he will forever be a memory in the hearts of those he touched.

Till we meet again Sir Ken Dodd, Sleep well.

Brett Williams

Brett Williams

KING OF COMEDY

Ken Dodd...what more can you say!

I miss our Doddy every single day.

No other comic can take his place.

Gentleman, a man of humble grace.

Onstage, nobody could ever compete.

Funniest person you could ever meet!

Comedy King, no argument there!

Only one Doddy, nobody to compare.

Master of Mirth, had the perfect act.

Exceptional talent, most others lacked.

Doddy, this book is from us to you.

Yours to read in your pastures new.

Mike Bartram

There's been nobody like him and there never will be. Rest in peace Sir Ken Dodd.

I thought, along with so many others, that you were just fabulous and you will be sorely missed. Thinking of Anne and all your family and friends.

Sending love

Carrina Rowe - Heswall, Wirral

Your great city of Liverpool will dearly miss you Doddy along with all the people in it who loved you like family. You will also be missed by all the people in the world you have made laugh over the years and I will miss you too.

You are a star back in heaven now Sir Ken, back home were you belong because earth only had you on loan. Remember to take good care of your new wings, keep your harp tuned and never comb your hair.

All my heart felt love and best wishes to Sir Ken (Doddy) Dodd.

Bob Picthall

A true gentleman with always a smile on his face. My daughter sings in the Liverpool Cathedral Youth Choir and we have seen Sir Ken and Lady Anne on many occasions here, always a pleasant word or smile and very courteous to all. Liverpool has lost a true entertainer, our family will miss your warmth and humour. Goodnight, God Bless Sir Ken.

Michelle, John, Abbie and Lucy Ewart Hughes xxx

Cont.

Sir Ken was an amazing person and showed us nothing but support and encouragement with everything we did. Ken was a master to learn from and we will be forever in his debt and grateful for what he did for us. Ken will always be in our hearts! Sending a big Abracadabra.

Lots of love

Danny and Steph

Amethyst

The Plan

I'm off to Southport, a short car ride.

A small bunch of flowers are by my side.

This wasn't my plan 2 short months ago.

My plan was to see the Ken Dodd show.

Doddy our hero, forever top of the bill.

I planned to see Doddy, I knew the drill!

To experience happiness, forget my cares.

Outside patient cabbies, waited for fares!

But I'm off to Southport with a new plan.

No Doddy to see, the world's funniest man.

At the Theatre I leave my flowers behind.

Nothing else here tonight for me to find.

As God in his wisdom had a plan of his own.

I now leave Southport, an early trip home.

Mike Bartram

Fan's Tribute

My sister and I attended Ken's funeral. On the day we worried a bit about getting inside the cathedral as we knew it would be very busy. On the morning my sister Sheila was looking for a handbag to go with her outfit (we dressed up and carried tickling sticks and our friend Sandra who is also a big fan made us all corsages for our lapels). So Sheila finds a little handbag and when she opens it up there are 3 tickets to see Ken Dodd at the floral pavilion in New Brighton. These tickets had been reserved for us by Ken and Lady Anne.

The last time Sheila had used this little handbag was when we had gone to see Ken so she decided she must take this bag with her. When we got to the cathedral early there were so many people there we didn't think we would get a seat but we walked in and one of the stewards asked us if we were family. "No, not family" we said "but we are the Diddy twins". The steward looked a little puzzled and said "oh, so you are big fans"

The rows of seats are full but he directed us to where there were three vacant seats left in an area near the altar. We think we have probably the best view ever. We sat with fellow fans, ordinary people like ourselves who had a genuine love for this man. The celebration of Ken's life that day was incredible. Moving tributes from the people who loved him. Jimmy Tarbuck, Stephanie Cole, Jimmy Cricket and author, producer and friend John Fisher and many more.

There were tears but there was so much happiness too on display from start to finish. What a send-off as the Diddymen followed Ken down the aisle to a standing ovation and

Cont.

rapturous applause. It wasn't until we got back to the car and Sheila opened her handbag and looked at the 3 tickets she had found that morning that she realised the seat numbers on the tickets "Row B" 16, 17, 18. We like to think that Ken reserved THOSE seats for us too.

Susan Callaghan

Susan & Shelia Callaghan

My Dad was the Manager/Chaplain of the Theatre Royal St Helens a number of years ago. Ken hadn't appeared there for a couple of years. My Dad booked him and it was a total sell out. As a great Doddy fan he said he was great to work with.... No great demands on booking and just genuine friendship grew. My Dad was there 6 months when the independent Methodist churches were running it. The stage manager was Mike Littlewood.

I bought my Dad a ticket to see Ken Dodd once. He sat in the audience laughing so much and at the break said to the gent next to him, 'my family won't come with me again' the man said 'I don't blame them!!!!'

We did go with him again, nearly every year!

Sue Stanworth x

50 years ago today (6/8/68) I met Ken for the first time when he was opening a TV/ record shop in Birley Street in Blackpool. Just a child at the time, I was a bit scared of the huge crowd that was right across the street and into Corporation Street. Ken was sitting at a table in the front window of the shop, signing records. I still have that record! Ken was so very welcoming to everyone and so kind. Many years later I asked him if he remembered that day and was amazed that he did. I'll never forget it. Bless him.

Sandra Wallace

Cont.

I saw Ken do his first TV show, his uncle Charlie ('he had played with Jack Hilton's band') told me, his nephew was appearing on a Saturday night, Ken came on and said 'I am the only member of our family to be able to eat a tomato through a tennis racket' he then sang a song, we met a few years later when he came backstage to see us, we have met many times since, and also at the Good Turns society where Ken was the President.

Geoff Ray

Blackpool Opera House (1971?) where Ken was the star for the summer season. Because of its wide aisles the Opera House could accommodate 87 people standing at the back of the stalls and 56 on the circle. Only when all of these spaces were occupied did "House Full" go up outside. It was up every night at second house during our holiday. So there we were, seated near the back of the stalls with people standing behind us. The show was fabulous, and it was almost time for Ken to come back on stage again. A door closed very quietly behind us, and I looked round.

The man in the red moggyskin coat quickly put a finger to his lips and winked. Ken was standing alongside some of his audience in full regalia and they hadn't noticed him! The orchestra started to play Love is Like a Violin, and all eyes were on the wings but nobody appeared of course. After about 10 seconds there was a sudden loud shout... Ken, slapping his Union Jack hat on his head and sprinting to the front then up the steps and on to the stage. What an entrance. What a genius. Audience helpless with laughter before he'd spoken a word.

Sandra Wallace

Your Poem

The Last Diddyman

Walking the sands for evermore.
I saw a Diddyman on the shore.
In Blackpool he walked all alone.
Liverpool lad, Knotty Ash his home.
But Knotty Ash now not the same.
I said 'hello' Dicky Mint his name.
Dicky all forlorn by the rolling sea.
He turned saying 'hello' back to me.
I saw a tear fall from his diddy eye.
Doddy I said would say 'not to cry'
On a deserted beach, lights so dim.
'It's time to go home' I said to him.
So home we went, Knotty Ash bound.
The last Diddyman I now had found.

by Mike Bartram, L25

The Whitechapel Centre

'Have you any loose change, please sir'?
'Got any 'odds' that you can kindly spare'?
Words from a young girl sat on cold stone.
Her scribbled message, it states 'no home'

In the cup by her side, I see coins are few.
Her eyes lack pride, and they lack life too.
Her words seem whispered in quiet shame.
It's not by choice that she begs in the rain

She sits on London Road in busy Liverpool 3.
Many homeless people there you'll sadly see.
Bus shelters or doorways become their roof.
The homeless on the rise, here's living proof?

My spare change I give, a 'thank you' is mine.
Young eyes peer at me which no longer shine.
As I'm walking away a sense of guilt I feel.
Support The Whitechapel Centre is our appeal.

Mike Bartram

whitechapelcentre.co.uk

Sir Ken Dodd obe

Oak House, Knotty Ash

The family and I would like to thank you all very much for your wonderful messages after the passing of their beloved Ken. The cards and letters expressing such great affection, indeed love, thanking him for his ministry of laughter and happiness for over 70 years have been a great comfort at this time. Also to read so many individual memories of his kindness when he enjoyed meeting people on and off stage throughout his life.

We hope the joy he brought will always be with you.

One life lived – many lives touched.

ANNE

Lady Dodd

Acknowledgements

Foreword John Martin
Introduction Shaun Gorringe
Editors Lady Anne Dodd & Mike Bartram
Front Cover artwork Lee Joyce
Front/Back cover design Oliver Harper (photofirstaid)
All digital images enhanced & edited for publication by Oliver & Jenny (www.photofirstaid.co.uk) they really worked their magic this time, thanks very much!
Compiled by Mike Bartram
Back cover picture Doddy fans: Brett Williams/Adam Small
The Liverpool Echo
The Blackpool Gazette
Radio Merseyside
Jon Bartram, Emma Bartram, Rachel Bartram
Book Layout & Design Mike Bartram
To all at **Grosvenor House Publishing** for their kind support, advice and not to mention patience given to me during this book's publication.

Cont.

Other books (all poetry) by Mike Bartram
Hillsborough 20 Years On...ISBN 9781906823153
Justice Call...ISBN 9781906823283
The Nightmare of Hillsborough...ISBN 9781906828498
25 Years of Hillsborough Pain...ISBN 9781906823979
Hillsborough Our Greatest Victory...ISBN 9781786238825
Road Safety and Awareness (In Memory of Bobby Colleran)...
ISBN 9781786238825
RoadPeace Poetry (Dedicated To Bobby Colleran)...
ISBN 9781786232410

All proceeds from the above publications are donated to various charities and good causes.

To every fan and friend of Sir Ken Dodd who made a contribution for this book a massive 'Thank You' without you our little tribute to the great man would not have been possible.

A sincere thank you to Lady Anne Dodd for giving her continued time, invaluable advice and support in the process of this book's publication.

Mike Bartram (dandy.77@hotmail.co.uk)

Tatty Bye Doddy...we love you and will never forget you!

Lightning Source UK Ltd.
Milton Keynes UK
UKHW020236031120
372663UK00007B/529